About the Au

Harriet Harman was born in 19ͻͻ ɑ̣̣ ̄ ̄ ̣
London. After studying Politics at York University she
qualified as a lawyer and worked at Brent Law Centre in
London, handling cases on behalf of community groups,
trade unions and tenants. From there she went on to be
Legal Officer at the National Council for Civil Liberties.
There she handled Civil Liberties cases, and Equality
cases under the Sex Discrimination and Equal Pay Acts
which had just come into force.

Harriet Harman's political career was a natural development from her concerns for feminism and civil liberties. She was selected to replace Harry Lambourne, who
was retiring from his Peckham Constituency. He died in
1982 and she was elected in a by-election at a time when
there was growing concern in the Labour Party to have
more women MPs. She was seven months' pregnant with
her first child. In July 1984, while pregnant with her
second child, she was appointed Labour Front-bench
Spokesperson for Social Services. Following the 1987 election she became Labour Front-bench Spokesperson on
Health. After the 1992 election she was elected to
Labour's Shadow Cabinet and appointed Shadow Chief
Secretary to the Treasury in Labour's economic team.

She is married to Jack Dromey, National Secretary in
the Transport and General Workers' Union, and they live
in London with their three children.

20th Century Man · 21st Century Woman

How Both Sexes Can Bridge

THE CENTURY GAP

Harriet Harman

VERMILION

LONDON

For Harry, Joe, Amy, and Jack.

Published in 1993 by Vermilion
an imprint of Ebury Press
Random House
20 Vauxhall Bridge Road
London SW1V 2SB

Catalogue record for this book is available from the British Library.

ISBN 009 1778190

Typeset in Baskerville by SX Composing Ltd
Printed and bound in Great Britain by
Mackays of Chatham PLC, Chatham, Kent

This book is printed on recycled paper.

Contents

Foreword

There have been many important books to tell us that marriages are breaking down, acres of newsprint to tell us that the economy is in the mire, and hours of television time devoted to politicians slugging it out in Parliament. The aim of this book is to assert that something must be done and to suggest solutions. There is simply no point in standing around wringing our hands. And there is no point, either, in men blaming women or women blaming men . . . or women blaming themselves.

As part of the research for this book we asked women and men to tell us what they felt about their marriage, their children, their work and their democracy. We talked to women from every walk of life and from different parts of Britain, but the message was the same. Men and women might live under the same roof, but they inhabit different worlds.

I am confident that women, whatever their class or race, will instantly recognise what I am saying. Men will recognise what I am saying too, but may find the message more uncomfortable. Because they need to change. At home, they need to change as husbands and fathers. At work they need to recognise that they are not *the* workforce – they are half of it. In politics, men will have to recognise that the demand is not just that men should speak up for women, as well as for men. That demand has been superseded. The change we need now in politics is that women must share power on equal terms with men.

Many people have helped me write this book. Over the past twenty years Patricia Hewitt, Anna Coote and I have developed our ideas together. Their help in this book has been immeasurable; without them it would not even have been started.

The House of Commons is a very different place today from when I first became an MP ten years ago. All the Labour women Members who have swelled our ranks have transformed the breadth and quality of debate, but I owe particular thanks for help on the book to Joan Ruddock, Alice Mahon, Dawn Primarolo, Tessa Jowell, Jean Corston, Maria Fyfe, and Marjorie Mowlam.

Carol Pearson kept the whole project on the road and was ever available to discuss ideas from beginning to end. Adrienne Burgess, Geraldine Brennan and Jenni Moore were important in ensuring that the text saw the light of day, as was Kate Mosse, who became involved at the last, but important stage. John Carr sorted out the new technology, The Institute of Public Policy Research allowed me to pick all their brains, particularly those of David Milliband. I am also indebted to the staff of the House of Commons Library for their highly professional help, and to Jo Keenan, Emma Hartley and Jo Rule. Deborah Mattinson and GMA Monitor, in conjunction with Field Search Services, conducted the interviews for the book. Thanks are due to Linda Elvin for quickly and expertly typing them up.

Kathy Sutton and Vicky Phillips were very helpful, as were many other members of the Labour Party. This book is not about the Labour Party, but my political home lies there partly because I believe it is Labour which provides the best hope for making the changes I argue for.

Gail Rebuck, Rowena Webb and the team at Random House were a joy to work with. My sister, Virginia Harman, my parents and Liz Bannister gave help at home, so that the practical business of being a parent did not completely halt the practical business of writing a book. Most of all, my thanks go to my husband Jack Dromey. Consoling a friend of ours whose marriage had broken down, he urged her not to blame herself. She was, he said, twenty-first-century woman trying to live with twentieth-century man. So the concept of the century gap was born.

Chapter 1
A Century Ahead

> ❛ *I don't regard myself as Anthony's wife. We're a partnership. Just because I say I don't work, that I'm somebody's wife, I don't have to add me to him. I'm a person in my own right, he's a person in his own right. We're a partnership, and that's it.* ❜
>
> Sheila, 41, has one son and lives in London with her husband, a welder.

Twenty-first-century women have arrived, a century ahead of time: ahead of the men to whom they are married, the employers for whom they work and the government which shapes the society in which they live. Women have not only staked out their ground in the family of the next century, they have staked out their ground in the workforce of the next century. Already their lives are centred both inside and outside the home. Ask them who they are and they tell you what they do: 'I'm a nurse and I have two children', or 'I'm an accountant and look after my mother.' No longer do they say: 'I'm somebody's wife.'

Women have left the twentieth century behind. To the majority of young women of all backgrounds today the role of lifelong, full-time, dependent housewife is neither an option nor an ideal. Women are in the workforce in almost equal numbers with men and, according to some forecasters, will by the end of the century be in the majority. Women are responsible for a substantial percentage of the family income. The paid work that they do is central not only to themselves and their families, but to the prosperity of the economy as a whole. For today there is no area – no industry, no public or private service – which does not depend on the work of women as well as that of men for its successful operation.

The shape of women's lives has been transformed, and has very much the same profile today as it will have in fifty years' time. In the middle of the next century, as now, women will graduate alongside men in equal numbers from the colleges and universities. They will find themselves with strong domestic and economic responsibilities and with their lives based both inside and outside the home. And the average young woman, who now gives priority to her working life by delaying marriage beyond her twenty-seventh birthday, is less likely to be living with her parents until she marries. She takes out a mortgage or consults the rental ads in the newspaper, and finds her own home. For women, the giant, transforming step has already been taken. The argument is no longer about whether it can or could or should happen. British women have taken their place in the outside world – for keeps.

A Century Behind

> ❛ I do most of the housework, because I still think that it boils down to the woman. He won't do cooking, cleaning the bathroom, the toilet – you know he wouldn't touch that. I would clean the cooker and things like that, clean the fridge out. He does do the Sunday meal and he doesn't mind hoovering. ❜
>
> Deirdre is in the final year of a psychology degree. She has three children and lives in London.

But at the same time the changes which must follow this social revolution have yet to take place. The world of work is still based on patterns which assume that all employees are men, and women who count themselves as equal citizens see few changes in democracy to reflect the changes in their lives. Women's entry into the workforce has not been matched by men's entry into the home. 'New Man' may have appeared on the advertisers' billboards and in the commercial breaks, but he has yet to put in a sustained appearance at home. Although men's involvement in housework and the care of their children is on the increase, many men consider the business of running the home to be their wife's responsibility, even if they are both working. Women have stepped forward into the twenty-first century – but men remain a century behind. The trends are there, but the rest of the revolution has yet to happen.

. Many men today want to play a greater part in family life, recognising that they are missing out on something important. But if family responsibilities dramatically reduce or eliminate their wives' wages, they are driven to make up the shortfall by working all hours and as a result active participation at home becomes less, rather than more, likely.

Women, struggling with their new responsibilities in the world of work, are becoming increasingly exhausted and angry too; they feel not so much that they have it all as that they are doing it all. Their husbands are more and more confused and displaced; they need their wives to work, as their own employment is no longer secure and, in any case, cannot by itself maintain their families. But they either cannot or will not respond, by participating at home at the same rate as women are participating at work.

> ❛ It made me really angry that he wasn't pulling his weight in the house. My marriage was OK while we were both working full-time and there were no kids at home. Once the kids came along, well, the money wasn't there so there was a bit of that and long hours. I suppose marriages break down because one partner is not pulling the same as the other. ❜
>
> Susan is married for the second time and has three children. She lives in Dumfermline.

The changes that have transformed women's lives and are expressed in the century gap are undermining relationships between men and women and causing marriages to break down. Too many men are still trying to play this new game by the old rules: still expecting the old levels of 'service' or trying to assert the kind of 'authority' that now looks completely out of date. Many women expect not only to give practical and emotional support to their partners, but to receive the same themselves. And when it is not forthcoming they petition in increasing numbers for divorce. The result is that many families are in turmoil. Vast numbers of marriages are collapsing, children often losing contact with their fathers, and fractured families sink into poverty.

Bad for business

The century gap is also taking its toll at work. Working practices are still shaped around forty-hours-a-week, forty-eight-weeks-a-year male breadwinners, supported by undemanding families and earning the entire family wage.

These assumptions, which were never entirely valid, are now hopelessly out of date. Today a wage sufficient to support an entire family is rarely paid to a single worker, man or woman. Furthermore, virtually half the workforce now consists of female workers with family responsibilities who, almost by definition, have no-one to support them.

Individuals are keen to work hard, but they need flexibility across their life span. The seven ages of man – and woman – require different levels of employment at different times. Young people can survive and even thrive on enormously long working hours, while older women and men may need to scale down as they approach retirement. The demands on time and energy made by the raising of a young family or by caring for elderly dependent relatives are substantial. But, in the modern world, the time span allotted to these activities is generally brief.

Women now spend fewer years pregnant or away from work looking after small children; most elderly people are self-supporting almost to the end. Yet entire working lives are destroyed and our economy cheated of some of its most valuable assets because for selected short periods women are forced to bear the important burden of family responsibility virtually alone.

The economy that will succeed in the twenty-first century is the one that can make the most of its human resources. Thanks to the century gap, we are not doing this. Such waste is a national scandal. Of course not all women want demanding jobs, but there are talented women, often expensively trained and educated, who, in order to fulfil their double role as carer and worker, are doing housework when they could be designing computers.

Bad for Democracy

The century gap also weakens democracy. The British political process is seen by many people as irrelevant and out of touch. This should come as no surprise. Look at the House of Commons – and at our town halls – and we see a political map more suited to a society with half its population behind the veil. Our 'representative democracy' is not representative at all. Women now regard themselves as equal citizens. They can vote and run for public office, they support their families and pay their taxes. Yet the decisions that shape their lives are still made, overwhelmingly, by men. Politics today is not only unrepresentative and fails to accord women a voice, but, like our working practices, it too is riven by the century gap.

This failure of our democracy to move with the changes in society exacts a high price. Half the voters, women, perceive politics – often rightly – as irrelevant to their lives and their concerns. If they vote it is out of a sense of civic responsibility, or because others fought for their right to do so, or even because their husbands vote. But many have no appetite for democracy; they feel no enthusiasm for the process. Their relationship with it is distant, and by and large they rule themselves out from deeper involvement. Emotionally they are disenfranchised – and that undermines and impoverishes democracy itself.

The quality of the decisions made is also compromised. Public policy affects the private as well as the public sphere. Yet Government, Parliament, local government and the civil service are all dominated by men, many of whom in their turn are comfortable with the public sphere but estranged from the private sphere. Too many are in exile from their personal lives. When they talk public affairs they miss out an entire, and vital, personal dimension.

Moving the Debate On

> *If I get married I wouldn't expect my wife to do it all. Years ago that was the thing, wasn't it? I mean, why should she have to do it all, especially if she's worked all day? Why should she have to come in first and start preparing dinner while the other half just sits around doing nothing and just eats it, puts the plate to one side and she takes it and washes up, comes in and watches telly with him an hour-and-a-half later, or whatever? It's not right, but it still happens and people accept it.*
>
> Brian, 24, lives with his parents in north London and works in an accounts department.

But if the century gap leads to broken marriages, economic inefficiency and political dislocation, the solution is not to try and bridge the divide by turning the clock back. The solution is to accelerate the changes, to complete the revolution. The century gap will be bridged when men and women participate in both the world of work and the world of home on equal terms; when our Parliament and politics reflect society as it is now, rather than as it was forty years ago.

Twenty-first century women are not prepared to sacrifice their relationships with their families – as men have traditionally done – nor are they prepared to sacrifice their working lives. Neither of these sacrifices are necessary. They will no longer be fobbed off by claims that the male pattern of a working life is the only possibility. For women have now been behind doors that once were closed to them; they have seen with their own eyes the 'make-work', the 'present-ism' and the 'crisis management'. They have decoded the jargon, seen women in jobs they were once told a woman could never do, and observed successful job-sharing schemes. Women know, with a confidence that they have not had before, that they are as good as men – as clever, as competent, as capable – and that there are new ways of doing almost anything.

The Twenty-first Century

How will the twenty-first century look when the social revolution and its consequent changes are complete? Politicians will discuss with equal confidence policy that relates to the public sphere and the private sphere, while ordinary citizens will find daily life and politics can happily be intertwined. Men will be as assured and as conscientious in their caring responsibilities at home as they are at work. And women will find their employers recognising that both they, and their husbands, wish to divide their life between home and family. It will no longer be possible to identify a person's gender simply by looking at the hours they work or their position in the hierarchy.

When men take a full part in family life our homes will be less of a battleground. Marriage will become a relationship of democracy, rather than a power struggle. When women are able fully to participate in the world of work our economy will be revitalised. And when, in equal numbers with men, they walk the corridors of power, the entire political structure will be refreshed; the outside world will relate to it in new ways and democracy will come alive.

A romantic picture? But there is no alternative – clearly things cannot go on as they are. It is neither possible nor desirable to turn the clock back. The emancipation of women cannot be reversed; and even if it was, the result would be total economic collapse. The only answer is to bridge the century gap by speeding up the process of change. Change is now inevitable, and to embrace it will prevent economic waste, avert political dysfunction and help men, women and children avoid much personal heartbreak.

It is happening slowly. Men's lives have in recent years become progressively more home-centred. Workers and employers all have a mutual need of, and capacity for, flexibility. Our democracy craves the active participation of all its citizens. Once, the 'demands' of feminism were seen primarily as 'doing women a favour'. Now they have become social, economic and political imperatives.

Banishing Guilt

Simply attributing blame for the current situation will not take us anywhere. We must now move beyond blame of both the 'women simply aren't up to it' and the 'It's all men's fault' variety. If the dislocations of the twentieth century are to be sorted out in the twenty-first we must bridge the century gap – and do so together. Women need no longer exist under a burden of guilt – for not being a good enough mother; for not making enough of things at work; for finding family responsibilities overwhelming, work frustrating, politics irrelevant. It is not women who need to adapt: their lives have changed a-plenty. It is the lives and processes around them that must now change.

Chapter 2

How We Reached the Century Gap

> *❝All the day-to-day jobs at home are down to me. I do every-thing – cooking, washing, ironing, finances, everything. I'm just more organised, I know where everything is. He doesn't do any-thing. It's probably my fault because I'm so fussy and like every-thing done correctly, so in the end it's just easier for me to do it.❞*
>
> Melanie, 35, lives with her husband and two chil-dren in Surrey, she used to be an estate agent and now works in a pub.

The housewife – the ideal, full-time, life-long dependant on her husband – has been the dominant image of women for much of this century throughout the Western world. The word 'housewife' – or rather, 'husewif' – first appeared in 1225. But the highly skilled agricultural and textile producer to which it referred, and who people the work of Chaucer, resemble a twentieth-century housewife as little as do today's women of the Third World, who labour, trade and support their families as well as look after the home.

From the fourteenth to the eighteenth centuries the term 'housewife' would have meant little, since it was only upper-class ladies who would not have been ex-pected to work in the world outside; nor, with full-time servants, would they have had to do any housekeeping. Indeed, an eighteenth-century English court register shows that, out of eighty-six married women, only one did not have a trade or profession of her own.[1]

The modern housewife, in her much narrower incarna-
tion, was, in Britain, largely a creation of the middle-class
Victorian philanthropists. Outraged by the 'immorality'
of female factory workers and the exploitation of children, largely as a result of the Agricultural and Industrial
Revolutions, they sought to create a safe haven for 'the
fair sex' and her children. And by the end of the nineteenth century, the idea that men worked to support their
families while women cared for them within the home
had firmly taken root. In reality this was a luxury for the
burgeoning middle classes only, but the ideal of what the
writer Coventry Patmore called the 'Angel at the Hearth'
characterised Victorian aspirations.

By the turn of the century, upper-class and wealthy
middle-class married women were likely to be cared for
by a selection of servants, and the day-to-day care of their
children was undertaken by nannies. But married women
at this level of society would be expected to manage and
organise the household, and to busy themselves with
charitable work. The majority of working-class women
still joined the workforce in their early teens, but even
though their standard of living would have been immeas-
urably improved by continuing in paid work after marriage, they started to stay at home to care for husbands,
children and other relatives. According to the sociologist
Ann Oakley, by 1911 only one out of every ten married
women was employed outside the home. Most of them
would have been in service, and were often employed
with their husband as a team: for example, cook and but-
ler, or housekeeper and gardener.

But that was by no means the whole story. Every generation has included women who have led independent
lives, and the last hundred years have been no exception.
As the housewife phenomenon gathered momentum, so,
too, did the rise of New Woman, the Bluestocking, who
petitioned for the right to higher education, who founded
colleges, who worked in medicine, journalism and a other
professions. Envied by some, New Woman was pitied too

– very often she was childless, or even unmarried. Teaching, in particular, remained the preserve of unmarried women who had to support themselves.

The decades passed and the housewife became enshrined as the symbol of feminine and social success. Pay structures and working practices had fallen into line and male responsibility was demonstrated daily by the husband going out to work to support his wife and family. He was now the breadwinner. The prevalent view was that a married women having to work was a 'misfortune and a disgrace'.[2]

But the loss of huge numbers of men in the trenches of the First World War, and the Depression years that followed in the 1920s, meant that from the 1930s there was a steady increase in women's employment even though the ideal of the housewife remained constant. During the Second World War when, again, female labour was essential to the wellbeing of Britain, married women were increasingly visible in the workplace, and by 1951 one in four married women was employed outside the home.

Late Twentieth-century Woman

> ❛ I think I'd work even if I didn't need the money. I was bored. This sort of time last year, I realised I could keep my house clean and tidy, I could get the washing and ironing done and I could do the things the kids wanted done. I had finally got it under control and I was beginning to want other things. ❜
>
> Lorraine from Sussex is 35 with two sons. She works part-time in a school for children with learning difficulties.

Now, less than fifty years later, the feminine ideal as a full-time, life-long housewife has all but vanished. Women had done so-called men's jobs during the Second World War, so the widespread nature of the ideal of the stay-at-home wife was partly an attempt to assimilate soldiers back into a civilian working life. It helped create the image of a new, safe world where everything and everyone had a place.

But the attempt to insist that a woman's place was solely in the home foundered, partly because it coincided with the arrival of washing machines, vacuum cleaners and other labour-saving devices. Shopping and cooking were transformed under the influence of supermarkets and pre-prepared foods. It was hard to accept that women should spend more time at home just as technology was taking much of the time-consuming drudgery out of domestic work at home.

> *I think being a mum means being a jack of all trades. When you are at home with the children you've got to be a person who sorts out difficult problems, children fighting and arguing. You try to teach them to compromise, try to get them to behave. You need to be a teacher when they bring their homework home and they need help. You've got to be a nurse when they're ill. You've got to be a bit of everything rolled into one as well as come in and cook the dinner and deal with the household chores.*
>
> Denise, 38, has three children and lives in Hull. She recently divorced after 19 years of marriage.

Then the notion of the housewife as ideal started to come under more direct challenge, first from the image of the superwoman and subsequently from that of the career woman. 'Superwoman' was a term coined by Shirley Conran in her books *Superwoman: Every Woman's Guide to Household Management* and its sequel *Superwoman in Action*.[3] She played the housewife at her own game – preparing the family's meals, doing the cleaning, shopping and ironing – but was still at work on time. In many ways, this was no more than working-class women had been doing for generations, but it brought into public consciousness the fact that women were capable of fulfilling more than one role at a time.

This super-mother/super-worker challenge to the housewife-mother ideal, and the implied criticism of women who did not work outside the home, led to attempts to defend the ideal. The housewife's activities were catalogued: far from being 'just a housewife', she was a homemaker. A feminist organisation called Wages for Housework tried to quantify a housewife's typical day in terms of what she would earn if her labours were financially rewarded.

By the 1980s the image of the superwoman had been replaced by that of the career woman. She was supposed to work all hours and serve pre-prepared food to her children.

Meanwhile, virtually unnoticed, the housewife had been creeping out of her house; she was heading single-parent families and wrestling with Social Security payments; she was working after marriage until her first child was born, returning to work after her last child had started school. And then her 'years out' had begun to shorten: she was working between the births of her children, and full- or part-time even while they were very young; she was being trained and educated and, though everyone thought she was still a housewife, the truth was that she was now an essential, paid worker in her own right. By the early 1990s the ideal of the full-time, life-long housewife had gone and women constituted half the British workforce.[4]

Twenty-first century woman

Housewife, New Woman, Superwoman, Homemaker, Career Woman – throughout the twentieth century women have been defining and redefining what it means to be a woman. Now, twenty-first-century woman has arrived; the synthesis of them all. She straddles the world of home and the world of work; deeply involved in both, indispensable to both.

It is diversity rather than conformity which charac-
terises the life of twenty-first-century woman. Although
life-long marriage remains both the ideal and the reality
for most women – it is estimated that 63 per cent of
women born in the 1960s will stay married to the same
man for life, even if not actually living together[5] – women
are living in different ways. Women head the majority of
the 26 per cent of British households which are single-
parent; women leave home and share with friends or live
in lesbian households; 17 per cent of women choose to
cohabit with partners, and 17 per cent live alone.[6] Children are being brought up within families of different
shapes and sizes, and men can no longer take it for
granted that their wives and girlfriends will want them to
stay under any circumstances.[7]

---

*❝ The early morning cleaning job, I did that for five years. I
didn't intend to do it for this long, but it suited me at the time.
Of course, it meant I was off out at five o'clock in the morning
and my husband was having to see to the kids in the morning
and I was a bit grumpy.*

*I gave up cleaning when I moved in with my second husband.
Now I work twenty hours in a chemist's shop, five mornings and
every other Saturday. I really enjoy it.❞*

Janet is 37 and lives in Ayr. She has two children of
her own and two stepchildren.

Women's working patterns are as diverse as their families. By autumn 1992, 45 per cent of women in employment in Britain were estimated to be working part-time
(that is, up to thirty hours per week) and 55 per cent full-
time. The average woman now spends approximately
thirty years of her life – often almost continuously – in
paid employment.[8]

Women work every conceivable type of 'shift': some
work evenings or early mornings or at weekends or
during the school term; others work nine to five; others

put in twelve-hour days six days a week. And these patterns change over their lifetimes. As one woman described it: 'I am a working woman with children ... when I was working part-time I felt the other way round – a mother who works ... but as time lapses, and you take on longer hours, you become a worker who's got children.'[9]

And what of the housewife, whose image has dominated for so long? She simply is not an option for twenty-first century woman. The young women of today do not envisage married lives entirely devoid of economic activity. Their mothers, after all, established the trend – with 95 per cent whose first child was born in 1960 returning to paid employment since.[10]

In America, Sharon Thompson's interesting study of 150 American teenagers has shown that virtually all the girls recognise that they will be in paid work for much of their lives and see work skills as a basis for their future autonomy.[11] Anne Machung found that almost all college women are now seeking high-powered careers – as well as husbands and children.[12] In Britain, Mansfield and Collard's study of sixty-five newly married British couples[13] showed that even women who anticipated career breaks to accommodate pregnancy could not imagine living for life 'on one wage', while members of Patricia Hewitt's Institute for Public Policy Research discussion groups (reported in her excellent book *About Time*) who were working limited hours to accommodate young families, commonly said that their 'careers were on hold' – even if, in reality, their prospects for real career jobs were slight.[14]

Unlike the housewife, who vehemently rejected the idea of paid work, or the career woman, who romanticised it, twenty-first-century woman's approach is pragmatic. Working women today view wage-earning as both a burden and a source of joy and pride, as men have long done. As Barbara Amiel, a senior political journalist on the *Sunday Times*, put it in a thought-provoking article in *Mirabella* magazine in March 1992: 'Only an idiot would say that life is lessened by the fact that, finally, women do have more choices. But only an idiot would conclude that choice is an unmixed blessing.'

Work is central to the lives of most twenty-first century women, for few now limit themselves to a 'little job on the side': a majority bring in 30–50 per cent of the family's total earnings and, increasingly, a small number of women contribute 50–100 per cent. For twenty-first century women it is not simply a question of *wanting* to 'have it all'; if the mortgage or rent is to be paid and the children clothed and fed, they *have* to do it all. Together with their husbands – and sometimes on their own – they, too, are now breadwinners.

Twentieth-century man

During this century of women's changing lives, what of men's? In Britain in this period men have been defined in one way only, as breadwinner. Sometimes it has been put differently – master of the house, head of the table, provider – but these have only been alternative ways of saying the same thing.

Two world wars played their part in exiling men from their wives and children. For while the concomitant social shake-up gave women experience of life outside the home, these same wars separated men ever more firmly from their loved ones and seemed to confirm that they were not indispensable to family life. Many men during this century have not been sole breadwinners any more than housewives have been purely housewives. But the concept of breadwinner as the male ideal has nevertheless dominated to such a degree that, until recently, a man who did no more than provide well for his family was considered, by definition a 'good' father and husband.

The world around twentieth-century man has changed dramatically; but while his position has changed, it has done so only slightly. 'Men are the laggards in the transitions now occurring – and in a certain sense have been so ever since the late eighteenth century,' writes Anthony Giddens.[15] 'In Western culture at least, today is the first period in which men are finding themselves to be men, that is, as possessing a problematic "masculinity". In previous times, men have assumed that their activities constituted "history", whereas women existed almost out of time, doing the same as they had always done.'

New Man

> ❢ *At one point she was working full-time nights and I was working full-time days. So when it came to taking the children to school and things like that, she would do it. Now I do all of that because I'm not working at the moment. A lot of my friends have said that I'm an idiot for doing it. They don't think I should be there all the time, especially my father. He thinks I should be free and easy because he was like that when I was born. He used to still go out two or three nights a week with the boys. But that's the way I am. My family comes first, no matter about other things. I deliberately have made myself the opposite to what my father is.* ❢
>
> Martin is in his 40s with two children. His wife is a nurse and they live in Plymouth.

The first sign that men's roles are consciously under review was the emergence, during the 1980s, of the New Man. By no means all observations about him are favourable: he is often characterised as a wimp, just as the career woman was at first designated a ball-breaker. But despite backlash articles and books, from writers such as David Thomas and Neil Lyndon, claiming that he is nothing but an ad man's invention, some New Men are appearing at the school gates and in the supermarket. The hostility of these writers, in claiming that the faults of the world can be laid at the door of feminism, highlights the strength of the antipathy some men still feel against women. Men feel threatened by a new form of masculinity, even though the determining characteristics of New Man are, as yet, by no means clear. The name New Man tells us little about him – only that he is not what has gone before. And just as, 100 years earlier, the particular bias of the person describing a woman of advanced views as a New Woman could render that term positive or negative, so today the term New Man is open to the widest of interpretations – and abuse.

Another problem about the image of the New Man is his frequent portrayal not as someone who wants to be in an equal partnership with a woman, but as someone who wants to be under the woman's control. Relationships in the twenty-first century will not, however, see women getting the upper hand as men used to. What is envisaged is a partnership on equal terms: man as neither wimp nor dominator. A power struggle in relationships will be replaced by democracy. Today, twenty-first-century woman is the genuine democrat. New Man is the partner in the democracy of relationships who has yet to arrive.

Along with the washing up, it is the balance of power within society and within her own marriage that twenty-first-century woman will expect to share. She may no longer tolerate her husband using the remote control switch to flick through the TV channels without enquiring what others in the room may want to watch, but neither does she wish to flick thoughtlessly through them herself.

The Double Life of Twenty-first-century Women

Despite work patterns structured by men for men, despite almost non-existent childcare provision, despite two recessions and lengthening dole queues, the number of women in employment has soared by nearly 20 per cent since 1979. This upward trend was clearly visible throughout the late 1980s and has not been halted by the most recent recession. Male employment is down by 6.5

per cent since 1975; female employment for the same period is up by exactly the same percentage.[16]

Furthermore, during the last twenty years the gap between the numbers of men and women in the workforce has narrowed almost 25 per cent. In 1975, for example, 63 per cent of women were defined as 'economically active', compared with 84 per cent of men; by 1991 the figures were 71 per cent for women and 88 per cent for men.

Today:

- 43 per cent of mothers with children under five have jobs
- 67 per cent of mothers with the youngest aged five to nine are working
- 75 per cent of those whose youngest child is ten-plus are working
- at all stages more women insist that they would like to work if only they could find jobs, training and/or adequate childcare.

It is because women's entry into the world of work has not been matched by men's entry into the world of domestic responsibility that there are difficulties.

Within the home:

- full-time employed women spend an average 102 minutes per day on routine housework and 107 minutes looking after pre-school children
- full-time employed men spend an average 35 minutes per day on routine housework and 44 minutes looking after pre-school children
- part-time employed women spend an average 188 minutes per day on routine housework and 73 minutes looking after pre-school children
- part-time employed men spend 49 minutes a day on routine housework and 37 minutes with their pre-school children

The 1992 British Social Attitudes survey found that over two-thirds of the women with full-time jobs took on the main responsibility for general domestic duties: 60 per cent prepared the meal every evening and 78 per cent did all the washing and ironing. Furthermore, women working part-time carried virtually the same responsibility for home and family as women who were not working: over 90 per cent of both groups did all the washing and ironing; 81 per cent made all evening meals and 82 per cent did all the household cleaning.[17]

A Century of Change: Women

So why do women's lives appear to have changed so much over the past fifty years and men's so little?

Control over fertility is one of the most important reasons for change. It is often mistakenly perceived as stemming only from the 1960s when the Pill became available. The Pill, in fact, merely continued the trend which had been in progress since the turn of the century: by 1890 the average number of children per family was 6.34;[18] by 1951 it had fallen to 2.18, and today it stands as 1.82.[19] This reduction in family size has released an enormous amount of time to women, a change further augmented by the increase in life expectancy.

A woman reaching adulthood in 1890 would spend four and a half years of her life pregnant, and more years breastfeeding and caring for her children. Since average life expectancy then was only forty-seven, women had relatively few years when they were not bearing and caring for children. But a woman reaching adulthood in 1950 would have spent, on average, just two and a half years pregnant, and her life expectancy soared to seventy-five years by 1951.[20] But many women, middle- and upper-class ones especially, would have been out of the job market until their youngest child left home. As for the girls of today, who will reach adulthood at the beginning of the twenty-first century, they are likely to spend less than two years actually pregnant. The majority of mothers will be working at least part-time once their youngest child is five years old, and since average life expectancy for women by the year 2000 is estimated to be in the region of eighty years, much of the next generation of women's lives will be spent in paid work.

> ❝ *I'd like to be married eventually. I'd quite like to have children, but I'd rather build a career first. I want to establish a career, and then I'd hope to go back to the same career after the kids, although maybe on a part-time basis. I will want a career, but I wouldn't want to block out my children totally.* ❞
>
> Nicola is 20 and a university student. She lives in Reading with her parents.

And because domestic appliances have reduced the amount of time that tasks in the home take – between 1961 and 1985 the length of time the average British woman spent on routine housework fell by some fifty-five minutes a day – there is slightly more time for other pursuits. Interestingly, the time spent on shopping and caring for children has increased over the same period.

Investment in women's education, too, has had an enormous impact on what they feel able to achieve. In 1950, when nearly half of all pupils left school at the age of fifteen, only a small minority of girls stayed on. In 1950 only 5700 of the 16,500 students in higher education were women, of whom a substantial number were doing teacher training courses.[21] By 1991, the percentages of men and women going into higher education were roughly the same – 13 per cent of women aged nineteen to twenty, as against 14 per cent of men.[22] Women are also much more likely to return to education later in life, and indeed the success of the Open University has in part been due to the 47 per cent of women who make up its average undergraduate intake.[23]

The participation of women of all classes in an increasingly wide range of jobs is of course directly affected by their level of education. The more qualified they are, the more years they spend in employment; they are more likely to return to work between births, after their last child is born and when their children are grown up. This is not just because of the financial rewards that come with careers that are valued, but also because of the level of job satisfaction. Women work not just to make ends meet, but because they want the fulfilment that a job can bring.

More recently, the marked decline in the ability of a single male wage to sustain a family has further altered women's lives. This has been due to many factors, including house-price inflation, expectations of higher standards of living, and what has been called the 'missing middle' – the decline in the number of jobs, many of them skilled blue-collar jobs in the manufacturing sector, which once paid the 'family wage'.

So over the last hundred years there has been nothing less than a revolution in all the areas of women's lives which have been of greatest significance to them. Furthermore, since many of these changes began several decades ago their impact is now widely felt and seen. Change has not only occurred, it is *seen* to have occurred; and the aspirations as well as the life structure of twenty-first-century women have changed accordingly.

A Century of Change: Men

These shifts have affected men's lives also, but not yet deeply enough to force a widescale re-evaluation of the relationship between their working lives and their home lives. Over the century men have become progressively more home-centred, due largely to a dramatic reduction in the average time they spend at work. Today's men work shorter hours every week, fewer weeks every year and fewer years overall, entering the workforce later and

retiring earlier. But, as Patricia Hewitt has pointed out, '
... the *shape* of men's lives has not yet fundamentally
altered. Men's lives are still a sandwich: education and
retirement, with full-time employment in-between.'[24]

Men's increasing home-centredness began to be
obvious after the Second World War. In the *Anatomy of
Britain* Anthony Sampson noted the 'crumbling of the
professional men's clubs' and observed that 'the misogy-
nist zeal which built the Empire and kept wives in their
place – that has gone'.[25]

> ❝ He wasn't very good when the children were younger, but he
> gave up smoking a few years ago and he changed completely
> because he couldn't bear to sit and do nothing if he wasn't smok-
> ing. So that's when he started to do all these hobbies and DIY
> and helping more. ❞
>
> Rosemary is 45 with three grown up sons. She works
> part-time as a dental receptionist and lives in Man-
> chester.

Men's leisure began to be more focused on the home.
They would bring in beer 'so they can watch the telly at
the same time', as a woman told researchers Young and
Willmott;[26] and the popularity of DIY grew. Men's participation in routine housework was, however, minimal.

Since the mid-1970s that has changed – a little –
though women still do four times as much housework as
men. Men's *attitudes* have certainly shifted – a growing
number of men under forty now claim to believe that men
are just as good with children as women, and the majority
of under-forties believe that men should help around the
house. It seems that the attitudes of the sons have moved
on from those of their fathers, even if in practice there is
still a long way to go.

> ❛ *If I get married I wouldn't expect my wife to do it all. Years ago that was the thing, wasn't it? The woman would have to do it all. But not now, because it would be my house too and I'd take a pride in it as well.* ❜
>
> Roy is 19 and lives with his mother in Preston. He works for the Post Office.

The time men spend on housework has more than doubled since 1961, although only from seventeen to forty minutes per day. Men, like women, also spend more time on shopping and caring for children. Fathers are now the most usual source of childcare for employed mothers, and on average look after their pre-school children for half an hour more every day than they did in 1961. These changes are small, but nevertheless significant.

However, although all these changes indicate some direct participation in family life, the move of men into the home in terms of time spent there still lags way behind the move of women into the workplace. In this respect, there is a clear century gap between the change in men's lives and the change in women's lives.

Now, in 1993, however, fundamental changes to men's working lives is inevitable – the kind of change which may well force a major reappraisal. The notion of a lifetime job is disappearing; skills which are highly sought after one minute can be redundant the next. And women are establishing themselves slowly but surely in a whole range of jobs which were once designated 'men only'.

Today men are faced with the fact that their wages alone cannot support their families adequately and that they may experience periods of unemployment or low-earning while they retrain or change careers.

Within their homes, too, men are finding that their lives are beginning to look very different. Quite often when they get home their wives are not there to make a meal because they are out working. And there are other, more important, changes. As women become more independent they are less likely to put up with what would have been tolerated in the past. As one man said when his wife, fed up with his persistent affairs, took their daughter to another city and filed for divorce: 'I didn't think it would mean I'd lose my *family!*'

All over the country men are losing their families – either through divorce or because women are deciding to have children without them: 90 per cent of single-parent households are headed by women, and the majority of men lose touch with their children. Increasingly, as women's involvement in the workplace grows and their responsibility to their families remains firm, men are feeling cast adrift – both from the workplace and from the family.

Looking to the Future

During any period of change it is to be expected that not all the elements will shift at the same rate. But as the pace of change for women continues to gather momentum, and as they face the twenty-first century daily more certain of their self-reliance, the gap between women and the men they are trying to live with has widened alarmingly. This century gap has built-in contradictions which are deeply destructive, both in terms of individual relationships and in terms of social organisation. For the vast majority of men are still living by the old twentieth-century-breadwinner-dependent-housewife model, with all the assumptions about control and value that this entails. Women, however, are beginning to live their lives in accordance with the very different demands now made upon them.

The century gap is also a gap in perception: the old twentieth-century structure on which men's behaviour is overwhelmingly based is no longer a reality for most families; while the twenty-first-century structure with its double set of obligations for women is very real indeed. Yet the twenty-first-century structure is either denied by men, employers and Government or is treated, at best, as a temporary blip in the statistics.

> ❛ I was in London two and a half years before I got married. I lived with friends, we had our flat and worked in the West End. We had quite an outgoing life and then to suddenly have to come back home every night and cook and clean for someone else was quite a big jolt which really I resented because I had been single until I was 28 and I have always done what I wanted to do, so to suddenly have to think about someone else was quite a big shock to me. ❜
>
> Pat is 40 and lives in London. Married with one son, her husband works as a builder.

The century gap, then, describes more than the obvious mismatch between two different approaches to work and family life; it also describes a clash between fact and fiction. For the nostalgic harking back to a way of life which (if it existed at all) is now long gone entails the widespread denial of life as it is being lived today.

Bridging the century gap means refocusing attention away from a past which we *thought* we had towards a very different future. This is important – not because, in so doing, we will make life nicer and cosier for everyone (though that will happen too) – but because our very existence as a two-parent, family-based society depends upon it.

Notes

1. Oakley, A., *Housewife* (Penguin Books, London, 1974)
2. Oakley, A. op. cit.
3. Conran, S., *Superwoman: Every Woman's Guide to Household Management* (Penguin Books, London, 1977) and *Superwoman in Action* (Penguin Books, London, 1979)
4. Hewitt, P., *About Time* (IPPR/Rivers Oram Press, London, 1992)
5. OPCS, 1992
6. General Household Survey, 1990
7. Segal, L., *Slow Motion: Changing Masculinities, Changing Men* (Virago Press, London, 1992)
8. Labour Force Survey, 1992
9. Sharpe, S., *Double Identity: The Lives of Working Mothers* (Pelican Books, London, 1984)

10. Hewitt, P., op. cit.
11. Thompson, S., 'Search for Tomorrow' in C. S. Vance's *Pleasure and Danger: Exploring Female Sexuality* (Pandora, London, 1989)
12. Machung, A., 'Talking Career, Thinking Job' in *Feminist Studies*, Vol. 15, Spring 1989
13. Mansfield, P. and Collard, J., *The Beginning of the Rest of Your Life* (Macmillan, London, 1988)
14. Hewitt, P., op. cit.
15. Giddens, A., *The Transformation of Intimacy* (Polity Press, London, 1992)
16. Labour Force Survey, 1992
17. British Social Attitudes Survey, 1992
18. British Social Trends Since 1990
19. OPCS Population Trends, 1992
20. OPCS Population Trends, Winter 1992
21. Annual Abstract of Statistics, 1960
22. Educational Statistics for the UK, 1991
23. Open University Statistics, 1989 and 1990
24. Hewitt, P., op. cit.
25. Sampson, A., *The Anatomy of Britain* (Hodder & Stoughton, London, 1962)
26. Young and Willmott, *Family and Kinship in East London* (Penguin Books, London, 1962)

Chapter 3

Marriage Across Two Centuries

> *I think the best thing about getting married will be the closeness with someone. You're like a team, starting out and doing things together. On the other hand, your partner has to put up with your moods, the way you're feeling, what you're going through every day, being with each other.*
>
> Shelika is 19 and lives in Bradford with her parents. She is training to be a nursery nurse.

Marriage has changed out of all recognition during the course of the twentieth century. During the first five or six decades it was still considered primarily a social institution – a state of affairs, not necessarily rewarding but none the less important – 'like having a job', says Giddens, 'that one does not particularly appreciate but dutifully carries on'. The ideal of mutual love between husband and wife was officially promoted but was only a secondary consideration.[1]

Men and women's lives were organised on the principle of separate spheres. In 1955 a survey of attitudes found that both sexes regarded the most important element of marriage as the efficient fulfilment of the roles of breadwinner for men and homemaker for women.[2] Although this emphasis on function over feeling fostered mutual suspicion (women often said that men only wanted one thing – sex – and men claimed that women were looking for a meal ticket for life) their expectations were, in the main, compatible.

The man, as breadwinner, paid his housewife's living

expenses and conferred social status upon her. Twentieth-century marriage was essentially seen as being a
man's gift to a woman who, although her family no longer
had to pay a dowry (as is still the custom in many parts of
the world today), needed to be married in order to be able
to live. As the French novelist and dramatist Henri de
Montherlant, who was born in 1896, wrote: 'The man who
marries always make the woman a present, because she
needs marriage and he does not.' De Montherlant was
known for his writings in support of masculinity, and his
tirades against what he saw as a feminised age.

It started to become acceptable for men to resent marriage and the women who had 'tricked' them into it. And
they blamed it for distracting them from more important,
'manly' pursuits. Open derision – hatred, even – of
women was sanctioned. Colin Willock's *The Man's Book*,
published in the late 1950s, contains no fewer than forty-
six jokes about women, all of them insulting, along the
lines of: 'No man regards his wife with pleasure, save
twice – in her bridal bed, and in her grave.'[3]

Working-class women usually had to work as well as
fulfil the role of wife and mother. But for middle-class
women marriage was almost a career; as the philosopher
Bertrand Russell once put it, 'their commonest mode of
livelihood'. Making a 'good marriage' was all-important.
And if they were considered lucky enough to find a husband, most women did feel deeply responsible not only
for the housework and the running of the home but also
for the success of the marriage itself. For, as many researchers have emphasised, in appointing women
managers of the domestic sphere men had handed over to
them not only the day-to-day menial work but also responsibility for the 'emotional work' of the family, too.

But, as Giddens and others have observed, you cannot
entrust your emotional life to someone else and expect to
remain completely independent of them. Certainly the
housewife was socially and materially dependent and
powerless; but, paradoxically, her power began to grow –
with the family as its seat.

When the household had been the centre of a productive system, as in the Middle Ages, male rule over it had been comprehensive. But the separation of home and workplace, plus the growing emphasis on the importance of emotional warmth between parents and children, caused a significant shift – until the core of that household could be seen to have moved from patriarchal authority to maternal affection.[4] And today, as we look towards the twenty-first-century, it is in women's hands that this power remains.

The Changing Shape of Marriage

> *When we were first married I was the kind to go along with everything he said instead of letting him know from the beginning that I was a person in my own right with things I wanted to do or things that I didn't want to do. He was very jealous. He always liked to have me there.*
>
> *I don't know whether it was my fault, but after a while I got fed up with doing everything his way and decided that I just wasn't going to do that. I wanted to do my own thing, too.*
>
> Shona is 39 and divorced with two teenage sons. She works full-time in a home for the elderly in Aberdeen.

Other key elements within the family have changed, too. Male-female relations have undergone nothing less than a revolution over the past thirty years, as part of what Giddens has called 'the generic restructuring of intimacy'.

Not only marriage, but all kinds of kinship relations are now under review. Blood ties had always been, in a sense, a Bill of Rights. But families used to be bigger – the average size of a middle-class mid-Victorian family was eight children – and since only half of the children born in eighteenth-century England lived to the age of five,[5] the emotional links between members of a family were weaker. As family size started to shrink and more emphasis was put on life-long bonds, the idea that blood was thicker than water gave family members enormous licence. Some behaviour was considered beyond the pale and rifts developed, but 'duty' remained the watchword.

Nowadays there is general agreement – in practice if not in theory – that love cannot be taken for granted, that it has to be earned. The 1991 Children Act gave this idea legal recognition for the first time: it accorded dependent children an identity separate from that of their parents, who must now not only care for them physically but nurture them emotionally and respect their views and feelings. 1992 saw the first case of a British child exercising its right to 'divorce' its parents. Nor can parents any longer simply assume that their adult children will provide for them in their old age; whether or not they do so will generally depend on the quality of the relationship forged.

'The term *relationship* meaning a close and continuing emotional tie to another, has only come into general usage relatively recently,' says Giddens. 'It refers to a situation where a social relation is entered into for its own sake, for what can be derived by each person from a sustained association with another; and which is continued only in so far as it is thought by both parties to deliver enough satisfactions for each individual to stay within it.' By 1971, when another survey looked at British expectations of marriage, both men and women were saying that the most important thing was for husbands and wives to 'like each other'.[6]

Today, the expectations of emotional fulfilment within marriage are even greater: both men and women now anticipate reciprocal nurture and respect, sustained communication and sexual satisfaction. The responsibilities carried by individual marriages became ever weightier as the structures which once supported them weaken. Young people move away from their home towns in

search of work or to study or travel, and in doing so develop value systems based on experiences very different
from those of their parents. Family networks are much
smaller and less powerful, and couples must now look to
each other for the kind of support that was once spread
around the family.

The duration of marriage has changed, too: as the
popular T-shirt slogan says: 'WHEN I SAID *TIL DEATH US DO
PART* I NEVER THOUGHT I'D LIVE THIS LONG'. People nowadays are living nearly thirty years longer than they would
have done when Queen Victoria was on the throne. The
average life expectancy of a boy born at the turn of the
century was 45.5 years and of a girl 49 years. But by the
year 2000 men are expected to live to 74.5 while women
can anticipate reaching 80. Marriage not only has to survive against a background of higher expectations, with
less support from the extended family – if it is to be lifetime's partnership it has to survive much longer.

Divorce Across Two Centuries

> *❝ I think you get to the stage where the kids have grown up and
> you think: 'I've got to sort myself out now.' Then the marriage
> broke down. I think my ex-husband is looking back on what he
> had and what he has got now and I think he misses the family,
> even though he lives with a girl between twelve to fourteen years
> his junior. ❞*
>
> Trudi, 35, lives in Brighton with her three children.
> She is working as a cleaner while she retrains in com-
> puters.

In this framework a growing number of marriages do
not survive. Britain has one of the highest divorce rates in
the world, with four out of every ten recent marriages
destined to end in divorce. Increasingly, divorced people
seem unwilling to remarry: the drop in marriage rates is

noticeable in all age groups, but especially among younger people. Second and subsequent marriages are even less likely to succeed. Forty per cent of second marriages end in divorce; and in recent years one in every four British divorces has been a re-divorce.[7]

But the difficulties between twentieth-century man and twenty-first-century women reflected in the divorce statistics alone: the number of people who never marry, though still small, is growing. Between 1970 and 1987 the proportion of women married by the age of fifty fell from 96 per cent to 83 per cent, and of men from 93 percent to 79 per cent.[8]

A *Guardian* article of 21 January 1993, discussing a recent report by the Joseph Rowntree Foundation, makes the point that there is an increase in the number of women under thirty who have never married.

> Figures from the 1991 census show the number of people who are divorced almost doubled over the previous decade to 2,690,000, 5 per cent of the adult male population and 7 per cent of women, compared with 3 per cent and 4 per cent in 1981.
>
> The number of women under 30 who have never married reached 3.8 million, a 12 per cent rise in 10 years, with more than 5 million men – 78 per cent of men under 30, compared with 70 per cent for women.[8a]

This reinforces the point that women today have often had a substantial period of independent life before marriage. You cannot re-impose dependency (through marriage) after more than a decade of independence.

In 1987 nearly 900,000 couples were cohabiting – an increase of 170 per cent on 1979 – and today the numbers are certainly higher. People choose not to marry for a variety of reasons, but this route is not a recipe for stability either: figures from Sweden, for example, show that cohabiting unions are six times more likely to break down than marriages.[9]

Although, clearly, there is a crisis in marriage now, it would be a mistake to look back to marriage between twentieth-century man and twentieth-century woman as some kind of ideal. There were many dissatisfactions inherent in it and, while divorce was rare, marital breakdown was not; unofficial separations and desertions were commonplace, and 'empty shell' marriages widespread. In 1971, Chester examined the increase in divorce between 1959 and 1969 in England and Wales and concluded convincingly that, whilst the divorce rate had increased by 100 per cent, the increase in marital breakdown was of the order of 65 per cent.[10] The suggestion was that levels of behaviour that might once have been tolerated within marriage were now no longer acceptable, and that women felt better able to cope financially on their own than they had in the past.

The Road to Divorce

People are certainly more able to divorce now, although it is simplistic to attribute the rise in the divorce rate merely to laws which make divorce easier to obtain. Certainly, short-term increases in the divorce rate often take place immediately after new legislation is introduced, but divorce rates in almost all countries – and especially in Britain – were on the increase well before the introduction of more liberal laws.

Furthermore, as all divorce researchers report, however easy the actual legal process is made, the road to divorce is a long and miserable one for most couples who, far from treating the matter lightly, generally endure years of problems before initiating divorce proceedings. Divorce is a final result of marriage breakdown, not its cause.

Certainly, divorce is more widespread today because it is no longer available only to the few; this past century has seen access to divorce gradually accorded to nearly everyone. Until the middle of the century the process and outcome of divorce were so expensive that only middle- and upper middle-class men, and a few women, could afford it. It was not until 1951, when for the first time the class composition of divorce petitions exactly paralleled the class composition of society, that divorce can be said to have come within the financial reach of most working-class men. And only recently has women's increasing involvement in the labour market, the provision of state-financed legal advice and representation, together with the availability of income support and a pool of local authority accommodation, made divorce a possibility for the majority of women.

Marital breakdown, then, is more widespread because so much more is demanded of that 'personal' relationship than has ever been demanded of it before; more visible because divorce is now almost universally available; and more relevant because its outcome is so very different from what it used to be. Fifty years ago a crisis in relationships remained largely a personal matter. Today, since it generally leads to divorce – that is, the breaking up of households – it has become an issue on the social and political agenda.

The Century Gap in Marriage

> 6 Well, obviously you think it's not going to be all roses, but you don't envisage the fact that you have someone else's washing, cooking and that sort of thing. 9
>
> Sandra is 40 with two children. Her husband and they live in the West Country.

At a time when so much more is demanded of marriage, it is being undermined from within – by the many conflicts arising from the century gap. Men and women approach marriage today with very different hopes and expectations, which they have great difficulty in reconciling. As Kate Mosse comments in *Becoming A Mother*, a great many women and men fail to share their notions of

the ideal family. Differences can remain unproblematical
until children arrive, when the reality of who is expected
to take responsibility for what can be extremely disap-
pointing. 'In retrospect, many women wished that they'd
looked beyond the birth during their pregnancies to
visions of how the nitty gritty of their lives as parents
would work. Both parties often make inaccurate or in-
complete assumptions about the other person's expectations.'[11]

More often than not, twentieth-century man regards
marriage as an institution – much as his father would
have done; while his wife sees it in a different light: to
her, it is a living organism. This mismatch is revealed
both in the statistics which chart men and women's very
different levels of input into marriage, and in the lan-
guage which men in particular use to describe their behaviour.

Researchers have frequently observed that, although
both sexes today claim to value 'togetherness' in marriage, it is generally only the women who talk about their
marriages in terms of 'we'. The men more commonly say
'I'. They don't feel bound to invest as much time or
energy in the actual relationship as the woman does.

In their recent study of marriage breakdown, Davis and
Murch noted that for most of the men marriage was still
regarded 'as a base – the haven from which they ventured
forth to face the world. They didn't give a great deal of
thought to maintenance of their base – except that they
convinced themselves that the purpose of all their outside activity was to provide the wherewithal to keep it
running.'[12]

Men have lower expectations not only of what they
must put into marriage, but also – and often like their
fathers before them – of what they expect to get out of it.
One of the Davis and Murch interviewees said: 'I was
going out with somebody but she [my wife] didn't know
anything about it – you know, sort of once, twice a week. I
don't think that would have broken my marriage up. I
was quite happy'. Another remarked: 'I didn't really want

a divorce. I was happy going on as I was. I mean, I wasn't a good husband. The fact is I was always out, always drinking, but I mean she never went without. It wasn't a wonderful marriage. I'd have carried on.'

The women of today entertain very different ideas, anticipating, as Mansfield and Collard discovered, 'an empathetic partner, a close exchange of intimacy which would make them feel valued as a person, not just a wife'. In this respect, as in many others, their expectations diverge not only from those of their partners but also from the expectations that their mothers had of their own marriages.

These different hopes and expectations reveal the extent of the split, with women emphasising the quality of the personal relationship (upon which, we know, modern marriage increasingly relies) and men's attention directed outside it. Men, as Hochschild observed, may be willing to give at work, but at home they expect only to receive.[13]

'Despite the promise of emotional fulfilment offered by modern marriage the gender gap of expectation in many of these newly-wed marriages was wide and men seemed either to be unaware of this or unable to accept it,' conclude Mansfield and Collard. 'Wives, in contrast, acknowledged the existence of the gap and hoped to bridge it'.

The Battle Over Housework

❝ There are certain things that she is better at than me. I shouldn't really say this, because it sounds horrible, but the ironing, the washing, making the beds, she's always done that. We have little arguments and inevitably it's, 'You don't help.' But I always say, 'I've got my jobs and you've got your jobs.' ❞

Tony, 38, from Birmingham is a manager with British Gas. His wife works for the local council. They have two children.

Who does what at home is now a key area of conflict in marriage. Among Mansfield and Collard's sample, fewer than half the couples shared the same view of how domestic tasks should be organised, with the century gap dividing them almost entirely along gender lines.

Women, increasingly conscious of their own dual role, do feel that their husbands should help them more. For example, 74 per cent of wives thought that the men could help with the shopping as compared to 5 per cent in Gorer's survey in 1955. But men's views are often more akin to those of their fathers' generation. In the same 1992 survey, 33 per cent of men claimed to believe in the 'traditional model of marriage', in other words that it was a husband's responsibility to earn the money and a wife's to look after the home and the children.[14] This view was echoed by almost all of Mansfield and Collard's male interviewees, only one in five of whom made more or less equal contributions to housework as their wives.[15]

These young men also placed tremendous emphasis on their wives simply 'being there' when they opened the front door. 'Men just get married so that they've got a mother,' one of Sharpe's interviewees commented sadly.[16]

❝ Like when anyone comes round it's the woman who gets up to make the coffee. It's generally expected and that bugs me. If we used to have people over for the weekend I would say 'What did everybody say then?' In fact, I'd say, 'I'm going to put a tape recorder down because I never heard a word.' You never have any social side because you're outside in the kitchen. Even if you have got a husband who helps it's still the women or the two women friends that are out in the kitchen and the men are gabbing on. Even when you sit down the children want something. It is just you that seems to get up and get it all the time. That's just a fact of life I suppose. ❞

Erica is 38 and lives in London with her husband and 4 children. She used to work in telephone sales.

To maintain this division of labour within the home, the majority of husbands, as all major studies reveal, utilise a wide variety of strategies. Some refuse outright – 'I've never done any washing in my life, so I don't see why I should now'; others profess incompetence – 'I can't iron'; and others invoke hostile belief systems – 'it's not a man's job'; while many adopt the tactics of passive resistance – waiting for their wives to ask for help, promising to do it later, castigating their wives for nagging and so on.

Increasingly, women now tackle these devices head on and a few do succeed in changing their partners' behaviour. But many fail and, if they wish to stay within their marriages, are forced to adopt strategies to manage inequality. Inevitably these put wives under enormous strain. Hochschild found that some women 'stop asking' and try to 'do it all themselves', often cutting important corners or becoming ill in the process. Yet others pretend that the men are doing more than they really are, thus concealing, but not eliminating, their anger and resentment. It is then not uncommon to find sex withheld as an unconscious punishment – sometimes by women, but also very often by men.

Many women today have neither the time nor the inclination to conform to the traditional image of housewife and mother, although a disturbingly high proportion of men still seem able to see them only in this way. This aspect of the century gap undermines marriage for, as Hochschild noted: 'The happiest two-job marriages I saw were between men and women who did not load the former role of the housewife-mother on to the woman, and did not devalue it ... [but] shard that role between them.[17]

Me, Breadwinner – You, Who?

> *⁶I never assumed that I would be in control of the money but –
> how can I put it – everything was for him. What was mine was
> his, but he liked the good life and when there was a financial
> crisis it was me that had to economise. He didn't, though. I
> could never say, 'I'm away shopping' and buy myself or the kids
> something, I always had to grovel and ask.⁹*
>
> Laura, 42, is divorced and lives in Fife with her
> daughter. She is a full-time secretary and works even-
> ings too.

Although still expecting their wives to be housewives,
the vast majority of men have, paradoxically, come to expect at the same time her financial contribution to the
household. One man in Sharpe's study even called his
wife a 'parasite' when she was at home looking after their
two very young children! But despite the fact that women
are expected to contribute to the family budget, that contribution is often not recognised. The concept of women
working for pin money is still very strong.

Most of Mansfield and Collard's young couples were
both working full-time, but there was 'invariably a gender
division of expenditure which consisted of husbands paying the rent or mortgage and major bills, and wives taking
care of the housekeeping expenses'. Even in those marriages where the income was pooled, the cost of keeping
'a roof over our heads' was attributed, 'evidently symbol-
ically', to the husband's earnings.

The downgrading, or denial, of women's financial input has a profound effect. For, as Clift and Fielding have
shown, it is only when women are *recognised* as making a
significant financial contribution to the family budget
that they feel able to require their husbands to contribute
significantly to the housework and childcare.[18] Furthermore, the perception of a woman's earnings as being 'for

the family' gives her greater bargaining power within it than if those earnings are believed to be for her own use as an individual. So it is common practice for the money to be defined as 'hers – to spend as she likes', when in reality it is used to buy things for the family or added to the housekeeping money.

Here the century gap between men and women's perception of wives' earnings is clear: while two out of three wives define their earnings as being 'for the family', fewer than one in two husbands see them in this way. And one in three husbands do not bother to find out what their wives earn at all, though they say they could if they wanted to. In such marriages the woman's financial contribution usually goes completely unrecognised, as Jan Pahl notes in *Money and Marriage*.[19]

Other means of making women's earnings 'invisible' are regularly devised 'especially by husbands', Pahl has observed.[20] Many researchers have noted that, where the wife's income is higher than her husband's, or where she becomes sole breadwinner, even for a short time, efforts are usually made to compensate him as if for loss of power. One woman who became the family breadwinner after years as a housewife had always accepted 'set housekeeping' from her husband, but: 'It didn't work because I never had enough money left.' But when the roles were reversed, she was forced to hand over her entire pay packet to him at the end of the week: 'Then he hands me back money for food for the weekend and bits for myself.'[21]

But women are growing less prepared to tolerate men's need to deny their wives financial input. The woman quoted above defined herself as 'a fool ... I don't think people believe I hand my money over.' And a young husband in the Mansfield and Collard study observed of his wife: 'She sometimes gets a bit despondent – how can I put it – that I don't ever say to her, 'We need some of your money to pay this bill', do you know what I mean? She'd like to be put into the position of paying the bill.'[22]

To continue to label the woman 'housewife' when she

is also breadwinner, or to continue to label the man 'breadwinner' when it is a title he cannot own and accords him a level of financial control he cannot justify, builds tension and contradictions into marriage. 'He likes to think he is still running the house and is the bread-winner, and my job is just an extra thing that I do because I want to,' observed a nurse of her factory worker husband.

❛ I could easily go down to Sainsbury's and buy a week's load of shopping, but I couldn't justify the fact that I wanted a new dress. I never argued about it because I felt I didn't have the right to argue. He wouldn't actually say 'No', he'd just make life really difficult.

If it had been my money I could have said, 'Well, I earned it – you can't tell me how to spend it.' But it was always his money. ❜

Jane, 36, is divorced and lives in London with her three children. A trained beautician, she now works as a cleaner.

Tied into the breadwinner-housewife stereotypes are important issues of control and respect. When a man sees himself as sole or main breadwinner – even when the housekeeping records show otherwise – it makes him feel that he has the right to ask for his needs to be put first. And when they are not – as today they rarely can be while his wife's time is increasingly taken up with fulfilling her responsibilities at home as well at work – he often feels hard done by and angry. As a number of studies have shown, much destructive conflict in marriage is triggered by husbands' beliefs that they are not being accorded the kind of respect due to a breadwinner. Pahl has shown a strong correlation between husband-control of finances and husband-control in decision-making – and a very sig-nificant association between male control of money and marital unhappiness. 'This,' says Pahl, 'applied equally to men and to women.'[23]

Male Absenteeism from the Home

Men, as has been shown, spend more time at home than they did fifty years ago. And many of them no longer behave like the average working husband of the 1950s who, according to a famous study of mining communities of the period, spent most of his non-working time in the garden or silently pottering about the house.[24] But even though some men do achieve genuine intimacy with their partners, many still have neither the time nor the inclination for intimacy; in marriage male absenteeism, both emotional and physical, is still widespread.

❛ *My wife is used to being on her own with the kids. I've just been away for six weeks working in London, for instance, but I'm normally in a factory so that's about 60 hours a week and I often work Sunday. It's by choice. I enjoy it. I have a good laugh. If you work hard you have a lot of laughs, you look forward to it.* ❜

Danny is 40 and married for the second time. He has three children and lives in Glasgow.

'I like it when you visit, Daddy,' said a three-year-old whose father – a plumber – worked such long hours that his child thought he lived elsewhere. And there are many men who, through commuting and work commitments, barely see their children from one weekend to the next – and sometimes not even then. According to an Equal Opportunities Commission survey, British men work the longest hours in Europe. One in two devotes more than forty-four hours a week to his work (not including travel time); one in four spends more than 50 hours per week working; and one in ten more than 60 hours. Many of these men are fathers with young children.

Even those who have free time do not necessarily choose to spend it with their families. On average, men spend 26.3 hours a week in leisure activities away from home. Women spend, on average, 21.4 hours away from home, but they very often have responsibility for children at the same time whereas their husbands are more likely to be with adult friends.[25] 'He was out all the time, either at the pub or golf or squash, keeping late hours,' said one of Davis and Murch's interviewees. 'I'm already a golfing widow,' a young wife told Mansfield and Collard.

It is not simply a question of physical absence, but also one of emotional absence. It is not enough for the husband to be there if his attention is not engaged by what is happening at home. In terms of the husband-wife relationship itself, men's emotional absence is legendary. 'He flops in front of the telly and tunes out,' explained a wife to radio agony-uncle Phillip Hodson. 'Then at bedtime he'll try it on with a kiss and a cuddle ... I've told him things have got to change but he just stands there and looks silly, saying, "What on earth do you want me to do?" How do I tell him I want him to, like, *be there*?'[26]

Who's Talking?

> ❛ At first I didn't actually want to get divorced – I only wanted to give him a bit of a fright. I thought maybe it would change his ways. I was prepared to take some blame, but he didn't seem to think that he was at fault at all. He just couldn't see it, even when it was pointed out to him. ❜
>
> Shona is 39 and divorced with two teenage sons. She works full time in a home for the elderly in Aberdeen.

Despite the fact that some couples communicate openly and well, the average man not only fails to express his feelings within marriage – 'I never say I love her; I don't know why,' said one of the Mansfield and Collard interviewees – he may not even share his thoughts. Another of the Mansfield and Collard sample said he hated to talk to his wife because it reminded him of his mother always 'trying to get things out of me'; while a third justified his preference for confiding in his mates in the pub with: 'They tend to be a sounding board, you say it but they don't take in what you say, as you are standing round in a circle having a laugh.'

Men's reasons for not communicating with their wives range from 'not wanting to worry her' or 'wanting to protect her' to actively wishing to keep her in ignorance. Quite a few feel their wives simply wouldn't understand – especially about difficulties at work. One of the Mansfield and Collard interviewees put it like this: 'She don't know what I'm on about half the time, so there's no point.' And failure to talk often goes with failure to listen. 'She talks. It's boring . . . I say "shut up!" was just one remark recorded by the study.

Failure to communicate is one of the reasons cited for divorce. 'Even before I went to a solicitor, if I said, "We need to talk" he'd get up and walk out of the flat,' a wife told Davis and Murch. 'He just wouldn't discuss it. And when I did come home and say, "I've filed for separation" he looked at me and said, "Well, why?" He seemed to have no idea what was wrong.'

'The only point at which many husbands will recognise that there is a serious problem with their marriage is when their wives go for divorce,' confirms Alison Hannah, a solicitor who has worked on divorce in East London and St Albans. 'They've failed to recognise that there's a problem because they don't take problems at home seriously. They don't really take anything at home seriously.'

Who Needs Marriage Most?

It is generally agreed that, of all divorced people, it is women with few or no qualifications who are the least able to survive, day-to-day, after divorce. Most are responsible for children, their skills do not earn them much money in the marketplace, they cannot afford good childcare, and they are unlikely to be in receipt of much financial support from their ex-husbands. Their best chance of life above the poverty line is undoubtedly to form a 'reconstituted family with an employed male'.[27] Small surprise, then, to discover that it is the ex-wives of unemployed working-class men who remarry most quickly, and that the ex-wives of employed working-class men are not far behind: within thirty months two out of five will have remarried.

Middle-class women who can support themselves and their families without a resident male wage are the least likely to remarry. Within the same period only one in four chooses remarriage.

For men, the scenario is reversed: very few unemployed men remarry within thirty months, and only one in four working-class men does so. But nearly half of all middle-class men have remarried within thirty months.

The inescapable conclusion is that women avoid remarriage if they can afford to, whereas men choose to remarry if they can afford it.

Men – the Real Losers in Divorce?

There aren't really any winners in divorce. I consider my husband lost in a way because the worst thing that has hurt him is losing the children ... well, he hasn't really lost them, but he considers that he has because he only sees them once a week.

Denise, 38, has three children and lives in Hull. She recently divorced after 19 years of marriage.

Women and children have traditionally been judged the losers in divorce, not least because they are more likely to suffer financial hardship as a result. The amount of money a man has to spend rises considerably in the first year after divorce, even if he continues to contribute to the costs of bringing up the children.[28] In many cases, fathers fail to take their financial responsibilities towards their children seriously, a problem considered so important in the USA that President Clinton and Vice-President Gore included measures against financially irresponsible parents in their election manifesto.

'[We will] promote tough child support through legislation and develop stricter, more effective methods to enforce it: crack down on deadbeat parents by reporting them to credit agencies so that they can't borrow money for themselves when they're not taking care of their children ... and make it a felony to cross state lines to avoid paying support.'[29]

In Britain, fewer than one in three absent parents (usually the father) makes regular payments, however small, in support of their ex-families.[30] It is hardly surprising, then, that a divorced mother's income is estimated to drop by as much as 30 per cent in some cases, depending on the number of children for whom she has responsibility.[31]

A recent survey published by the National Council of Women of Great Britain showed that after divorce 88 per cent of women take on the main responsibility for maintaining contact with friends, neighbours and family, including their husband's family.[32] The message is clear: when their marriages end, men are cut adrift from their families.

The most significant loss is of contact with their children. Within two years of divorce more than a third of the children in question are no longer in touch with their fathers. Over the ensuing years, many more drift away gradually, particularly those who remarry and start new families; for those who do keep in touch, contact is often sporadic. After ten years, over 50 per cent of divorced fathers had lost contact with their children altogether.[33]

> ❛ *Now, if I said to him, 'You can come back on the condition you stay at home with the kids and I'll go to work', he would do it. He realises that he was really out of order the way he acted; but if it had been suggested to him years ago, no way would he have reversed the roles. There's nothing he would like better now than to come back, but we're divorced and that's it.* ❜
>
> Val, 38, is divorced. She lives with her three children in London and works early morning shifts in a garage.

In their search for replacement families, men may choose partners who already have children and join that ready-made family, or they may have more children of their own. But, as many men acknowledge, it is difficult to replace being with one's first family as they grow up, sharing their day-to-day lives in an ordinary way. They can phone every week, see each other every weekend, but it's never the same.

It's not surprising, therefore, to discover that statistically it is men more than women who regret the decision to divorce; one in three of the divorced men in Davis and Murch's study[34] claimed that they wished they had remained married to their initial partners, while half of the men in Wallerstein and Blakeslee's sample, interviewed ten years after their divorces, felt the same.[35] Of the women, despite the poverty, despite the loneliness, despite the sheer struggle of working, paying the rent and managing the children, only one in five expressed regret about choosing divorce. They felt that what they had gained in independence and self-respect outweighed the material disadvantages.

Although a small proportion of ex-wives actively try to obstruct the relationship between divorced fathers and their offspring, most are keen to maintain it – and many take no issue over sporadic or non-existent maintenance payments in order to keep the father visiting the children for their sake. But divorced parenting – especially for the non-resident parent, which most of the men are – is problematic. Moreover, the father-child relationship during the marriage was often so remote that it is no surprise when it breaks down after the marriage is over.

Men's remoteness from the children of their former marriages is a direct result of the century gap. Men's limited contribution to the daily lives of their children during marriage leads many people to believe that they have no value within their families other than as breadwinners, even though study after study shows that children benefit from close, loving relationships with their fathers. From this it is but a small step after divorce to refusing to pay when you feel you are not getting anything back, and to believing that you really don't matter much to your children. If during your marriage your wife was, effectively, both mother and father to them, why should this state of affairs not continue?

Going it Alone into the Twenty-first Century

Twenty-first-century women find themselves faced with difficult choices. A very few are lucky enough to find partners willing and able to share with them the roles of career and breadwinner which they themselves must now take on. But if the rest wish to stay married they must often pay an enormous price: they can accept men's lack of participation and drive themselves nearly into the ground in their struggle to do it all; they can severely limit the size of their families in order to cope better; or they can continually engage with male resistance and in the process wear themselves and their marriages down.

The alternative is to opt for a single life. This, too, is a struggle and, though many ultimately take this step, only a small number do so without regret. For a few women, this last choice may involve the decision never to have children – though increasingly most do not see why this should be so.

The number of women choosing an independent existence is liable to increase as women become more and
more able to support both themselves and their families.
'What is going to happen to marriage and childbearing in
a society where women really have equality?' wondered a
Princeton demographer in 1986. 'The more economically
independent women are, the less attractive marriage
becomes.'[36]

A 1982 study of 3,000 single people, quoted by Susan
Faludi in her book *Backlash*, found that women earning
high incomes were almost twice as likely to want to remain unwed as women earning low incomes.[37] And another study, carried out in 1991, discovered that one out
of four lone parents *felt* financially better placed than
before – most commonly because the money coming into
the household was now theirs rather than the absent
partner's.[38] Solicitor Alison Hannah reports that, for
many women in low-income families, the ability to control the family budget is a strong incentive to becoming
or remaining single – even if it means living on a lower income: 'The woman wants to control the budget. She's
better off even on a low income, like Social Security,
because she's controlling the budget herself.'

'The unpalatable truth – certainly unpalatable to most
male politicians,' observe Davis and Murch, 'is that our
high divorce rate arises from women's economic freedom
to do without their husbands. It is not easy for them, but
it is just about possible.'[39] Although increasing numbers
of women are electing to go forward into the twenty-first
century without husbands, this does not mean that they
live solitary lives. Most have children or other dependants; some cohabit; others have live-out lovers.

But the majority, once they have taken control of their
lives, keep that control in great measure. In 1991, 30 per
cent of children were born outside marriage and 89 per
cent of all single-parent families with dependent children
are headed by women. Furthermore, 31 per cent of lone-
parent families consist of a woman who has never married, commonly with no more than one child.[40] 'Will we

soon have a matrilineal society?' asks sociologist Duncan Dormer, pointing out that 'in countries with high rates of relationship dissolution, a substantial proportion of children will be brought up by their mothers alone for much of their childhood'.[41]

Most twenty-first-century women hope not. The vast majority wish to share the workplace and the home with men whom they like and respect – but on new and equal terms.

❛I think a woman would make a very good man really! I think men are hopeless, in general. I know they work hard but their work ends at work, unless you've got an exceptional one who perhaps comes and does the housework. I know, because I haven't. I think women are on 24 hour call out and always will be. He has helped when I am nearly dying with the flu bug or something but generally it is really down to me.❜

Daphne is 35 and married with two children. She works part-time in a hospital and lives in Kent.

Notes

1. Giddens, A., op. cit.
2. Gorer, G., *Exploring English Character* (Cresset Press, London, 1955)
3. Willcock, C., *The Man's Book* (Edward Hulton, London, 1958)
4. Ryan, M., *The Cradle of the Middle Class* (Cambridge University Press, Cambridge, 1981)
5. Mosse, K., *Becoming A Mother* (Virago Press, London, 1993)
6. Gorer, G., *Sex and Marriage in England Today* (Cox and Wyman, London, 1971)
7. Marriage and Divorce Statistics, HMSO, 1989
8. HMSO, op. cit.
8a. *One-Parent families: Policy Options for the 1990s* (Joseph Rowntree Foundation, York, 1993)
9. Dormer, D., *The Relationship Revolution* (One Plus One, London, 1992)
10. Chester, R., *Divorce in Europe* (NIDI Martinus Nijhoff, Leiden, 1977)
11. Mosse, K., op. cit.

12. Davis, G. and Murch, M., *Grounds for Divorce* (Clarendon Press, Oxford, 1988)
13. Hochschild, A., *The Second Shift* (Viking Penguin, New York, 1989)
14. British Social Attitudes Survey 1992
15. Mansfield and Collard, op. cit.
16. Sharpe, S., op. cit.
17. Hochschild, A., op. cit.
18. Clift, C. and Fielding, D., *The Balance of Power* (Lowe Howard-Spink, London, 1991)
19. Pahl, J., *Money and Marriage* (Macmillan, Basingstoke, 1989)
20. Pahl, J., op. cit.
21. Pahl, J., op. cit.
22. Mansfield and Collard, op. cit.
23. Pahl, J., op. cit.
24. Denis, H., Henriques, F. and Slaughter, C., *Coal Is Our Life* (Eyre and Spottiswoode, London, 1956)
25. Planning for Social Change Survey, Henley Centre, 1992
26. Hodson, P. *Men* (Ariel, London, 1984)
27. Maclean, and Eakelar, *Children and Divorce* (SSRC, London, 1983)
28. OPCS: The Consequences of Divorce, 1984
29. Clinton, B. and Gore, A., *Putting People First* (Times Books, New York, 1992)
30. Bradshaw, J. and Millar, J., 'Lone-Parent Families in the UK', DSS Report No. 6, 1991
31. OPCS: The Consequences of Divorce, op. cit.
32. National Council of Women in Great Britain, 'The Superwoman Keeps Going – Understanding the Female Web', 1992
33. *The Family Way*, IPPI
34. Davis and Murch, op. cit.
35. Wallerstein, J. and Blakeslee, S., *Second Chances* (Corgi, London, 1990)
36. Otten, A. T., 'Deceptive Picture' in the *Wall Street Journal*, 25 September 1986
37. Faludi, S., *Backlash* (Chatto & Windus, London, 1992)
38. Bradshaw and Millar, op. cit.
39. Davis and Murch, op. cit.
40. OPCS Population Trends, Autumn 1991
41. Dormer, D., op. cit.

Chapter 4

Bridging the Century Gap in Marriage

> ❛ I suppose marriage was a joint announcement that we were going to stay with each other for a long time. I think we wanted some public recognition of that. I expected to have a very good friend and someone to sort of love and cherish me, and someone I could love and cherish back forever, really. It was a nice feeling that you would have to make a big effort to get out of it if you wanted to, and I don't. ❜
>
> Helen, 35, is a TV journalist. Her husband runs a design company. They have two children and live in London.

Despite the fact that the divorce rate is rising, lifelong marriage remains the aspiration of the vast majority of men and women. It is not that people don't want marriage – the problem is that the century gap is causing marriage to fail for a growing number of people. The ideal for bringing up children is two happy and fulfilled partners; if that is not possible, then two divorced parents continuing to have an amicable relationship and sharing responsibility for their children is the next best thing. So the question is: what can be changed to bridge the century gap in marriage?

Dr Jack Dominian, director of the marriage research body One Plus One, believes that the current level of divorce in Britain is 'mad for the couples, mad for the children, mad for society'.[1] A common response to the rising divorce rate is to suggest that we change the law relating to divorce. But making the actual process of divorce more difficult cannot resolve the problems that lead to the situation in the first place. For, as we have seen, the relative ease or difficulty of divorce is only one small element in the current increase in marital break-down. The major underlying cause is the transformation of marriage from a relatively short-lived formal contract, well supported by the extended family, to an isolated, complex, dynamic personal partnership which must endure for an unprecedented time and stand or fall by the quality of the intimate relationship.

> *The children were the main losers, because they have been through unnecessary heartache. They have seen a side of life which – especially if you are very young – I don't think it's nice to see.*
>
> Trudi, 35, lives in Brighton with her three children. She is working as a cleaner while she retrains in computers.

Divorce itself is, in a sense, merely a symptom of wide-spread and growing dissatisfaction and unhappiness within marriage. As marital researchers have pointed out, many of the problems associated with divorce – depression, ill-health, behavioural and learning difficulties in children – are in evidence years before a marriage actually breaks up.[2] The whole process has huge implications for the nation's health. After divorce, men and women are especially vulnerable to suicide, accidents and alcoholism. Children from dysfunctional families suffer more psychiatric illness than children from settled home environments and are more prone to addictions and stress-related illness in adulthood; they are also likely in due course to have failed marriages themselves.

Marriage breakdown also damages the national purse.

Collapsing relationships cost Britain, as a society, a fortune. In 1988, for example, we spent £1.4 billion (£27 million a week) on the welfare and legal costs directly attributable to divorce and separation, while it is estimated that British companies lose £200 million every year through absenteeism and impaired efficiency resulting from marital breakdown.[3]

While men and women try to sustain marriage across the century gap, marriage is doomed. What we need now are new structures to set marriage in an entirely different context and so reduce some of the key areas of conflict within it.

Turning the Clock Back?

> ❛ *I expected to have my own house, kids, my wife not to work. I'd be the breadwinner, or whatever. I wasn't saying that she should stay in the house. My second wife, now she's more like my own Mum. She's happy in the house. If I'm off working on a Sunday, she likes to get up and do the washing and ironing and that, and then go over to her mother's on a Sunday afternoon and she has her dinner there. So it's a good day for her as well.* ❜
>
> Danny is 40 and married for the second time. He has three children and lives in Glasgow.

Throughout the world, women's participation in the workforce is associated with their increasing dissatisfaction with marriage. As the statistics reveal, it is the most 'traditional' couples who are currently the least likely to divorce – those, for example, with strong religious beliefs or who do not live together before they are married.[4] Such marriages are not necessarily characterised by a high degree of mutual satisfaction – but they are marked by complementary expectations concerning men and women's roles.

So, would one way of cutting the divorce rate and

bringing men and women's expectations into line, and reducing some of the conflicts expressed in the century gap be this: to turn the clock back to the time when women were housewives and men breadwinners? And, if so, in whose interest would this reversal be?

Digby Anderson, Director of the Social Affairs Unit, is one of many proponents of such a strategy. He suggests that turning the clock back would require – beyond making divorce itself more difficult – the 'ostracising' of divorced people, 'different' education patterns for boys and girls, 'massive' cutbacks in state support for one-parent families, and 'restructuring of the taxation and benefits systems'.[5]

❝ I've got friends that say, 'Well, if I say that, he'll go off and not speak to me.' So I think, 'So what? For goodness sake stand your ground, you're part of this relationship. I think they think almost back to Edwardian days. Even in this age they don't know how much their husbands earn. ❞

Sheila

That would be the beginning: to attempt to bridge the century gap by reforming public opinion until everyone thought as they did at the turn of the century. It would require a massive propaganda campaign, as well as the severing of media links with much of the world lest enlightened values in other places 'contaminated' our system. Sexual shame, religious fervour, belief in the innate superiority of men ... all these ideas would have to be reinculcated into the population. As in many countries today where women still cannot vote, the principle of universal suffrage would have to be rescinded.

To suggest that women must again view the world from the kitchen window would simply not be acceptable to the British people. Even if it were logistically possible outside a totalitarian state to reverse profound changes that have been underway for decades, few people would want to return to institutionalised first- and second-class citizenship.

But if women are less satisfied with marriage in general, they are far more satisfied with the rest of their lives, according to surveys. The National Council of Women of Great Britain reports that 79 per cent of women aged between sixteen and thirty-five see 'getting on at work or finding employment' as a major goal, while only 50 per cent are concerned with having any – or more – children. Just 13 per cent of women of child-bearing age think that a women needs a child to be fulfilled – only 25 per cent of mothers actually think this. Extended choice has made women happier with their lot in general, as Julie Burchill noted in her novel *Ambition*.

> Yes, some of us will get ulcers, and some of us will crack up, and some of us will screw up our domestic situations, and some of us will end up at forty with a cat and a cook-in-the-bag cod-in-parsley-sauce dinner for one and wonder if it was worth it. But more will be happy and more women will be fulfilled than ever before . . . BECAUSE IT WAS OUR CHOICE![7]

Attempting to bridge the century gap by turning the clock back would also have direct and profound implications for the economic health of Britain. If work of half the workforce was withdrawn wholesale, the economy would simply collapse. Furthermore, employers could not remain competitive if they paid the remaining (male) workers sufficient to support entire families to the standards now expected.

In many other ways, too, attempting to turn the clock back would be bad for business. Half a century of investment in human resources would be wasted: 46 per cent of our new graduates are women.[8] And girls have overtaken boys at GCSE and A-level examinations: 41 per cent of girls leaving school in 1992 had five or more GCSE passes, as against 35 percent of boys; while 27 per cent of girls leaving had A- and S-level passes, as against 25 per cent of boys.[9]

If the century gap within marriage continues to widen

– or even remain constant – our family structure and the health of the nation will disintegrate further. The only possible answer is to move the clock forward through adjustments to working practices and social structures, to new expectations of marriage.

Men Contributing More

❝ I'd like to marry somebody bubbly who could get on with most people. I wouldn't expect her to work, but if she wanted to then that would be fine with me. OK, if we could afford to and if she wanted to stay at home, then fine. We'd just have to manage on one wage. But I wouldn't expect her to stay and look after the kids if she didn't want to. ❞

Tyrone, 23, lives with her parents in Cambridge and works in the post room of a small company.

What must men do to narrow the century gap in marriage? They will have to relinquish the position of breadwinner in fantasy as they have done in fact, acknowledging women's real contribution to the family as co-breadwinners and co-carers. They will have to recognise their interconnection with and importance to their children. Then they will feel able to celebrate their need of family life, and the joys and satisfactions they receive from it.

They must begin to take more seriously what goes on within their homes and accept that becoming a husband and becoming a father – if they choose to take these steps – will change their lives in fundamental ways. Within the family they must dramatically increase the time they spend on household chores and childcare; and they must exercise within their homes the rules of common courtesy and respect which they practise at work.

> ❝ *I knew marriage would change things. I was free and easy, out every night with the boys, and when I got married everything changed dramatically and it was hard because we had no money. The idea was that the wife would have children, the wife would stay at home all the time and look after the children and that would be her job. But financially we didn't have high enough earnings, and she wanted to work anyway. So we decided we would split it down the middle and take it in turns to look after the children and everything.*
>
> *We started off with nothing, we had nobody to help us at all. With both of us working like we have over the years it's been hard, but we've got a nice house and we're just about keeping it together. Mostly it's good fun.* ❞
>
> Martin is in his 40s with two children. His wife is a nurse and they live in Plymouth.

Men must talk more with their children and their partners and listen to what they have to say. They must genuinely pool resources with their wives and relinquish sole financial control. They must cut down the hours they spend at work or in leisure activities outside the home and encourage their partners' work activity instead. And, for the short time that their families are young, they must give up the idea of having much time to themselves – as women have always had to do.

Some men, of course, have changed little. But others are already moving in that direction – looking for more flexible working patterns, spending more time in their homes and taking on more household tasks, becoming more closely involved in their children's lives and openly wishing for closer involvement still.[10] Lynn Segal has asserted that 'it is quite simply not in men's interests to change too much, unless women force them to',[11] and other writers have echoed this view. But women are not now, and are never likely to be, in a position to 'force' men to do anything. Certainly, within the family, men and women are so intimately connected that change in one cannot, in the end, fail to affect the other. Women have done as much as they can; the active, fundamental and enduring changes upon which the bridging of the century gap depends can now come only from men.

Why Men Will Change

Men will adapt – are already changing – because it is in their own best interests to do so. As outlined earlier, they could once expect to retain the services of their wives and the obedience of their children whatever they did. But that is no longer the case. Women are voting with their divorce petitions, moving their husbands out, moving themselves out at the rate of 100,000 a year; and they are questioning the traditional value of the past. Do families really need the sorts of fathers that they themselves had?

And, by and large, public opinion is with women. It is not simply that they have drawn back the curtains from the window and are looking out, but that everyone else is looking in. Good fathering is starting to be praised and valued.

> *There are still men who do not want to push a buggy. Possibly because they think it's a bit cissy. My husband always pushes it when he goes out. My father for instance never ever pushed a pram but he pushes his grandchildren.*
>
> Pat is 40 and lives in London. Married with one son, her husband works as a builder.

Intimately connected with the changes in the home that are obliging men to begin reviewing the situation are changes in the workplace. These are already revolutionising men's attitudes towards working women in general, and will change them further. For when he is threatened with redundancy, the wife might be crucial as the new breadwinner.

Given the high level of unemployment in the Britain of the early 1990s, twentieth-century man is under obligations which he is not in a position to fulfil. Fewer and fewer men can provide enough to sustain their families on their own. In this climate few men can feel confident about remaining employed continuously throughout their working life.

And when a man can no longer deliver, he might find his wife – who had put her own working life on hold for his – becoming resentful. Women are not the long-suffering, ever-supporting angels of Victorian novels. Schooled to value men's breadwinner capabilities, having kept their part of the bargain many women rebel when their husband fails to do the same.

> *Being married changes your life. I like the company. There's less money, though, and I've had to work hard in the shop. Having a woman changed things, I wasn't in the pub so much or out with other blokes. It changed for the better, though. When you lift the paper, people are getting divorced all the time. We've been reasonably happy, though, for twenty-five years.*
>
> Joseph is 41 and runs a greengrocer's shop in Edinburgh. His wife works part-time. They have no children.

So, democracy, equality, openness and power-sharing must be the new values in marriage if it is to endure as an institution into the twenty-first century. For continuity and stability, in providing a clear and consistent framework in which to bring up children, formal or informal marriage has not been bettered.

Furthermore, when worrying that one out of every three marriages ends in divorce, it is easy to overlook the corollary: that two out of every three marriages remain solid. Research published in the *Journal of Marriage and the Family* suggests that fewer than one in ten of those could be deemed 'unhappy'. As the celebrated anthropologist

Margaret Mead wrote: 'No matter how many communes anybody invents, the family always creeps back.'

Notes

1. Dominian, Dr J., interview in *Daily Mail*, 2 December 1992
2. Dominian Dr J., Mansfield, P., Dormer, D. J. and McAllister, F., *Marital Breakdown and the Health of the Nation* (London, One Plus One, 1991)
3. *Marriage and Partnership* (London, One Plus One, 1991)
4. Population Trends, HMSO, 1990
5. Jones, J., 'Tougher Divorce Laws Urged to Bolster Family' in *The Independent*, 13 July 1990
6. National Council of Women of Great Britain, 1992, op. cit.
7. Burchill, J., *Ambition*, (London, Corgi, 1989)
8. Educational Statistics for the UK, 1991
9. Statistics of Education, 1991
10. For example, Russell, G., *The Changing Role of Fathers* (Queensland, University of Queensland Press, 1983)
11. Segal, L., op. cit.

Chapter 5

Children in the Century Gap

❛Having children changed my life in every way. The body no longer works the same way physically – you don't get sleep any longer and really you just have to laugh when you think back to those days when you were at work. You don't know what it is like to be tired until you've got kids, and yet you keep going and you discover extra jobs you can squeeze in so that you buy them all these wonderful things and see their little faces light up. You're tired and you're perpetually broke and everything, but it's wonderful.❜

Lorraine from Sussex is 35 with two sons. She works part-time in a school for children with learning difficulties.

Century gap tensions can lie dormant until children arrive. At that point century gap problems between men and women, and between women and work, emerge unmistakably.

The woman, who has been out to work and has been financially independent experiences a huge change when she is then at home with a child. The man who has shared financial responsibility with a working wife finds he suddenly has to work longer hours to make more money at just the time when his wife wants him to be home more to help her with the child.

It is the arrival of children which exposes the century gap and it is they too, who suffer its effects.

Childhood has always been effected by the shape of men and women's lives and in particular the economic demands on men and women. Indeed childhood is, in many ways, a modern concept. Before the turn of the century it was not viewed as a separate, important stage through which boys and girls passed before puberty; children were small adults, and throughout the preceding centuries had been expected to shoulder adult responsibilities, as they still are in many countries today. Eleanor, the wife of Louis VII of France and subsequently Henry II of England, inherited the Duchy of Aquitaine from her father in 1137 when she was barely fifteen years old; Edward, the only son of Henry VIII, acceded to the throne in 1547 at the age of nine. In the seventeenth century, childhood ended at the age of about seven or eight. And, as is still acceptable today in countries such as India, girls of all classes were frequently married and pregnant by the age of thirteen.

Until the twentieth century the relationships between parents and their children varied from class to class. Middle- and upper-class children were, by and large, cared for by servants, tutors and nannies. They would not be expected to work, but the children of the working class were part of the workforce – and one of the benefits of having many children was that there was labour to use or to sell.

For most families before the Industrial Revolution the home was not, for the most part, separate from the workplace. Even up until the First World War, the working-class home typically consisted of only one or two rooms. Everyone lived and slept together.[1] There was no separate place where mothers looked after their children away from the father and, until the Factory Act of 1891, which prohibited the employment of women for four weeks before and four weeks after childbirth, when the majority of working-class women became mothers the fact was barely noticed by their employers. Parenthood, like childhood, did not exist as an institution. While the parents were working, children might be looked after by older sisters and brothers until they too were old enough to work alongside their mother or father. Men who had trades, such as blacksmiths and carpenters, often took on their sons as apprentices.

But by the middle of the century the appalling working conditions in mines, factories and mills led to attempts to protect first children, then women, from inhuman exploitation. The 1842 Mines Act, which was the first piece of protective labour legislation for women, made it illegal for them to be employed in collieries. Two years later, the 1844 Factory Act took the radical step of classifying women of all ages with children and other persons in need of protection. Further legislation limited the hours that women could work and laid down age limits on child labour. It was moral indignation that carried much of this legislation through, led by influential politicians of the day such as Lord Shaftesbury: 'The moral effects of the [factory] system are very bad; but in the female they are infinitely worse, not alone upon themselves, but upon their families, upon society; and, I may add, upon the country itself. It is bad enough if you corrupt the man, but if you corrupt the woman you poison the waters of life at the very fountain.'[2]

Another crucial step was the evolution of the modern school system, which gradually extended the amount of time for which working-class children would be unavailable to join the adult workforce. Children of the upper and land-owning classes had long received education from private schoolmasters and governesses, but the 1870 Education Act established elementary education for all children. It was followed in 1902 by an Act providing a state system of secondary education for all. Children were starting to be viewed as a distinct group.

The mortality rate declined from the middle of the nineteenth century, although by the last decade of the century life expectancy was still only 47 years for women and forty-four for men.[3] However, infant mortality – death in the first year of life – fell significantly towards the beginning of the twentieth century. As each child came to be seen as irreplaceable, family size reduced accordingly, from an average of eight children some fifty years earlier to approximately four in the decade 1890–9.[4]

But, as Ann Oakley points out in her classic history of

the transformation of women from workers to housewives, Victorian legislation was instrumental in separat-
ing men and women from one another and men from
their children.

> 'If industrialisation caused the removal of the child from
> society by the school, then it caused a similar change in the
> structure of the family. With the separation of the family
> from the economy came withdrawal of the family from
> society, the domesticity of women and the idea of the home
> as a private place – a refuge from the public world of work
> and sociability.'[5]

Much emphasis came to be placed on the importance of a
mother to her child, largely through the work of psychol-
ogists and sociologists from the beginning of the twentieth century, peaking in the 1940s and 1950s. In *Housewife*, Ann Oakley examines the development through
psycho-analytic theory of the concept of motherhood.
She shows how the works of Sigmund Freud, the
American anthropologist Margaret Mead and the influential child psychologist John Bowlby had a lasting
effect on the way motherhood came to be viewed. Substantial research was used to bolster the new theory that
women should be at home caring for their children
because it was in their own – and their children's – best
interests. A treatise published in 1947 blamed most contemporary ills on women's deviation from their proper
gender role, and asserted that childbearing and childrearing represented for women 'almost their whole
inner feeling of personal well-being'.[6]

By the 1950s, therefore, the expectation was that a married woman would stay at home, bear children and look
after them until they were old enough to marry in their
turn. Children's needs were, almost for the first time in
history, viewed as paramount. As well as their day-to-day
needs, mothers also started to be seen as responsible for
the emotional health of their children. John Bowlby wrote
extensively on the importance of mother–infant bonding,
and in his study of juvenile delinquents in 1944 concluded
that a significantly high proportion had experienced
separation from the mother or mother substitute.[7] The

prevailing view was that it was essential for children to be with their mothers for as much of the time as possible. Good mothering was nothing less than twenty-four-hours-a-day mothering. More was expected of the mother than ever before; as Jane Price notes in her witty book *Motherhood: What It Does to Your Mind*: 'Society, having handed over the entire responsibility for mothering to women, can afford to have unreasonable expectations of what good mothering is.'[8]

At the same time, men of all classes were perhaps less involved in the day-to-day lives of their children than ever before. Their role was that of breadwinner. But as we have seen, this ideal started to be challenged. By the 1970s a man's wage was not necessarily enough to support a wife and family. Women wanted to work and to care for their children, too; by 1981, 18 per cent of mothers with children under five worked part-time, and 6 per cent worked full-time. The most recent figures show that 43 per cent of mothers of pre-school children now work, 13 per cent of them full-time. And 59 per cent of mothers with dependent children up to eighteen are now employed.[9] Mothers have moved from one century to the next, leaving their partners behind them.

Having Children Makes a Difference

❮ Basically, because I'm at my desk an hour before the children are ever going to school, there's no way I could take them. It's the same with picking them up. Things like swimming I'll try and do when I'm around, but because of our circumstances it's very one-sided, as I am reminded by her frequently. When you have a row, that's one of the first things that comes out – 'I'm always around with the kids'. But then we all calm down, and we know why things are the way they are. ❯

Robin, 32, has two children and works in the City. His wife is a P.R. Consultant. They live in Kent.

Women's lives are transformed by the arrival of children; men's lives are barely changed. Having children can be the moment when new fathers' and new mothers' lives set off in opposite directions, exposing the gulf between twenty-first-century woman and twentieth-century man and altering forever the relationship between women and men in employment. Governments, institutions and employers do not acknowledge or respond to these changes adequately.

> *❜ Nowadays if you marry a chap from university, someone who's always been on a similar career path to yourself, and then suddenly you are not on it any more, it changes the power in the relationship. ❜*
>
> Emma is 38 and a radio producer. She has a daughter and lives with her husband in Edinburgh.

What has happened over the past twenty or thirty years is this: men and women reach the end of their educational life with roughly similar qualifications – GCSEs, City and Guilds, a university degree and so on. They work for a few years, marry or live together. They both carry on working until the arrival of children. Then it is usually assumed that the woman will take care of them. Research shows that the majority of women want to look after their own children during the early years. In any case, most men earn more than most women, so it seems to make financial sense for her to be the one to stay at home or to reduce the hours she works.

Whether or not women return to paid employment after the birth of a baby, it is they who in almost all cases assume responsibility for the smooth running of the household. Men may help, but women put themselves in charge. It falls to women to sort out the childcare, to deal with domestic crises, to liaise with the school, and to be there when the children are ill or the childminder is on holiday.

> ❝ I remember when one of them got chickenpox – they couldn't get it together, they had to get it on separate weeks – so I was off one week and then I went back. Then whoops! Off again! I felt guilty for taking so much time off and felt it was unfair on the company. I think I asked my husband if he could take some time off, but I can't remember what he said. Anyway, he never has taken time off to take them to the doctor or whatever. It's always me. ❞
>
> Deirdre is now in the final year of a psychology degree. She has three children and lives in London.

After the arrival of children, women have to learn how to organise their lives differently and to think about many things at the same time. It is not the same for men. Women spend a huge proportion of their time with the children when they are young; men on average spend as much time out of the house as they used to before. Women seek work which is flexible and fits round their domestic responsibilities; men continue their so-termed 'real jobs' full-time. There are, of course, exceptions to the rule, but this is how the majority of families function.

> ❝ Having children changed my life drastically. I don't think I realised the total commitment. I thought about the glamour side of it, babies and the lovely buggies and got carried along there. I wouldn't be without them, but you tend to have this wonderful image of this little family going out and having nice family days, and then all of a sudden the excitement of everyone coming round stops and you're just on your own with the baby in your daily routine.
>
> He's quite a good father, but like most men in the 1990s he's never there. He leaves very early and he comes in really late, or he's away. He's got time for them when he's got time. When he's at home, he has got time for them. ❞
>
> Melanie, 35, lives with her husband and two children in Surrey. She used to be an estate agent and now works in a pub.

Women adjust to a different world, where men's domain remains the world outside the home, the world of work. They have yet to share the responsibility for children that they will have to do in the next century. This is the century gap in the context of families with dependent children.

The 1992 winner of the *Good Housekeeping* Women of the Nineties Award reflects the dual form of women's lives. Lesley Woodward was not a company director or a high-flying executive but a thirty-five-year-old breast care sister from Hull caring for mastectomy patients as part of a job-share. Sally O'Sullivan, editor of the magazine, wrote: 'Success 90s-style means balancing a job in among other equally important but previously under-rated elements in life – home, family, voluntary work, socialising, a hobby, travel – in whatever proportions they personally fit.'[10]

❛When I was off work and I'd say I was a Mum at dinner parties, people glazed over. I mean it really is the way it happens. You can see them discounting you because you're not part of the working economic scene. Here I am producing the next generation, and most people aren't grateful at all! You are definitely made to feel that you have chosen to have a child and that is your luxury and why should everybody pay out towards it. I've had rows with people at work who object to paying taxes towards education for children and their health ... oh yes, I find myself fighting that crusade quite a lot.❜

Helen, 35, is a TV journalist. Her husband runs a design company. They have two sons and live in London.

Changing from a couple into a family is an enormous step, as Kate Mosse says in *Becoming A Mother*, ' ... the transition from parent to non-parent is probably the most fundamental step we will ever take.'[11] Most people become parents, yet the fact is not sufficiently recognised by Government, local government or employers. Coping with children is seen as a private matter to be handled within the confines of the home. Work patterns do not reflect school hours or accommodate the school calendar. Childcare is viewed not as a matter for national policy but as something to be bought privately. Financial problems are seen as just one of those things when you start a family.

Children represent not only the future of their own family; they also represent the economic future of Britain. In Western cultures people define their desire to have children as fulfilling their personal goals, not as a means of furnishing society with its trainees, bus drivers or future student nurses. It is not seen as a contribution to the wealth of the nation when women conceive and bear children. Yet without sons and daughters there would be no generations ahead.

So why is childrearing held in low regard? Why must women choose between 'real work' on male terms, or combining motherhood with a job that does not match their economic potential and qualifications? As the century gap narrows, it is to be hoped that taking time out of paid employment to care for small children will come to be considered as valuable an occupation as any other in society. Campaigns to press for parental leave provisions will gather strength, to bring Britain into line with the rest of the European Community. Initiatives of this kind will help bridge the century gap between mothers and fathers.

Beating the Biological Clock

Aware of the difficulties ahead, some women postpone pregnancy for as long as possible. That way, they can first establish themselves in terms of work and identity. Delaying childbearing is one way of trying to cope with the problems of outdated employment patterns.

A recent *Options* magazine survey of fifteen successful women under the age of forty showed that only one – Liz McColgan, the twenty-eight-year-old Olympic and Commonwealth champion – had a child. For the other fourteen, who were aged between twenty-six and forty, their success stories so far excluded children.[12]

More women than ever before are now having children in their late thirties. In 1965, the number of married women having their first child at the age of thirty-five and over was 9,362, which represented 11 per cent of all births to women in that age group. In 1989, although the number of married women having their first child at thirty-five or over was only marginally higher – 9,871 – it now represented 20 per cent of all births for that age group.[13] Increasingly, women are delaying starting their families until the last possible moment.

In the past there were strong medical reasons not to delay pregnancy. The risks of chromosomal handicaps, such as Down's Syndrome, increase with age: the risk for a woman of thirty is 1 in 800; it goes up to 1 in 350 at thirty-five and to 1 in 100 by the age of forty. In addition, women's fertility begins to decline in their mid- to late thirties, and there were likely to be more complications at the birth. There was also a higher incidence of forceps deliveries and caesarian sections. But medical advances have now helped reduce these risks, and in fact two surveys – one in 1986 and one in 1990 – claimed that healthy women over thirty-five were now no more likely to suffer stillbirth or perinatal death than younger women.[14] Women are therefore no longer considered unusual or foolhardy to wait until their thirties before embarking on pregnancy.

> ❛ My mother-in-law stopped with us. I was expected to look after her as well as the kids. I had all the cooking to do and the housework, although she did all her own washing. When she came the kids had to share a room as well and that meant constant arguing, and she was always niggling away at the kids. After the divorce I have never seen or heard from her from that week to this. ❜
>
> Aileen lives with her second husband and one-year-old baby in Ayr. She has two older children.

A social consequence of delaying childbirth is that older parents lead to older grandparents. By the time a couple get round to having children, their own parents might well be in their late sixties. If this pattern is repeated for more than two generations, the grandparents – if still alive – may be in their seventies or eighties and too frail to play an active role in bringing up their grandchildren.

According to the 1991-2 British Social Attitudes Survey, 57 per cent of mothers with children under twelve still rely on a relative to look after the children when they are at work, and that is often the grandmother.[15] In the Institute of Public Policy Research paper *The Family Way*, the authors note that '... the proportion of the population aged 65 and over has risen from 10.9 per cent in 1951 to 13.2 per cent in 1971 and 15.6 per cent in 1987. This represents an increase of more than 2 million people aged 65-plus since 1951.'[16]

So delaying childrearing may mean a daughter or daughter-in-law will have to care for a dependent adult as well as for young children. Current figures suggest that 20 per cent of married women or women living with partners were carers, of whom 6 per cent were looking after a parent, 4 per cent looking after a parent-in-law and 4 per cent looking after another relative.[17] So postponing childbearing could have a long-term impact on family life and mean that more women have to stay out of the workplace longer than they would if they had children earlier.

And some women only have one child, hoping that it will mean less difficulty in balancing home and work. As Hilary Land said:

> When confronted (and I choose the word deliberately) with the possibility of having another child, I was frightened by the prospect. Exactly why, I do not fully understand. All I will say is two things: first, that I had realised how precarious my financial situation would have rapidly become had I wanted another child and had wanted to take as much maternity leave as I had taken (and felt I needed) the first time. Second, being a mother is about having a dependent. How, then, do mothers (or the child's principal caretaker) make room for other things they want to do, and how is a balance struck?[18]

Post-feminism

In the last few years, post-feminism – as it has been labelled by newspapers and magazines – has emerged. It considers the anguished debate about balancing children and a career, men's lives versus women's lives, as the death throes of 1960s' feminism.

According to the *Guardian*, Post-feminist woman can be recognised thus:

> She's young, ambitious, believes herself to be the equal of a man but is wily enough never to call herself a feminist. She'll play it by the boys' rules and win. She feels no loyalty to other women, makes no attempt to ease their way in the world. Sisterhood is not in her vocabulary ... The PFW is largely acceptable to men – you can treat her like a man, sexist jokes and all.[19]

The post-feminist argument has more converts among younger women without children because post-feminism offers no analysis for – or answers to – the challenges that children bring to women's lives. But most women will reach a point when they want to have children and want their children to occupy a central position in their lives.

Post-feminism takes us no further forward from the position where children are rendered invisible, and mothers downgraded at work. As the barrister Helena Kennedy wrote recently: 'Motherhood is like some skeleton kept in the cupboard ... In the legal profession it is certainly more acceptable for a male counsel to explain his late arrival because of a car breakdown than it is for a woman counsel to invoke the illness of her children's nanny.'[20]

Post-feminism may have some attractions when a woman is twenty-four with a good career and plenty of time ahead. It is easy, too, from that vantage-point to question the commitment of female colleagues who rush home to attend a school concert or deal with a domestic crisis. But things look very different at thirty years old with two children under five. Then 'playing by the boys' rules' is no answer for women – or for children. Women who try to play it by the boys' rules at that stage will not win. And neither will their husbands and children.

Wanting Children

In 1991, there were 699,200 live births in the UK.[21] Parents, of course, will say that their children are a source of love and happiness to them. They also mention frustration, anger, worry, embarrassment, guilt and expense. But the anguish of many childless couples is testimony to the importance that most people place on having children.

In a recent *Good Housekeeping* interview, couples struggling with infertility problems had this to say:

> There's something magical and unique about the pure exchange of love between parent and child. I needed – we both did – to have a child.
>
> *Matthew Fort from West London*

> I remember being in a supermarket once and seeing a pregnant woman struggling with a door. It sounds awful but I didn't want to help her open it – I wanted to smash it in her face.
>
> *Wendy Stafford from Kent*[22]

People want children for a wide variety of reasons, and men and women's reasons are often very different from each other. As Beatrix Campbell points out in her eloquent book *Wigan Pier Revisited*, motherhood confers status on young women who have little prospect of obtaining fulfilling employment.

> ... unemployed girls who've never experienced economic independence are doing the only thing they can – having babies, either getting married or not ... They never consider an abortion, often don't use contraception. They want kids. Of course they do. There isn't anything else. Being a mother has a certain status after all, it makes you a grown-up person.[23]

Men, as Yvonne Roberts has pointed out, still often want children to prove that they are responsible members of the community, that they are in some way 'real men'.[24] Most simply feel that their lives will be enriched by parenthood.

According to a research study carried out in Aberdeen, pregnancy is a time of great togetherness for most couples.[25] The researchers found that the men cared for their partners and often took the lead, 'talking' for them, planning for the future and so on. But once the babies had been born, the picture changed dramatically: the men became relatively silent and non-participative. It was now the women who did the talking and who were obsessed with their babies and those of other mothers.

> ❛ I would have liked more time off at the birth. With Emily – the first one – I had a week off because it was in August and it was quiet, but in December I didn't have any time off at all. The baby was born and I went back to work that afternoon. I know it sounds a bit blasé, but it was the second birth and it was very quick – in and out of hospital in a couple of hours. Well, my wife wasn't, but I had a lot of work and I just had to go in. ❜
>
> Robin, 32, has two children and works in the City. His wife is a P.R. consultant. They live in Kent.

As Kate Mosse suggests, the experience of pregnancy is always different for the mother-to-be and the father-to-be, however close they seem. Accepting this, and feeling confident enough to enjoy the pregnancy in different ways, means that many couples do enjoy waiting to become parents. Others become aware of the century gap all too soon.

A pregnant women is emotionally and physically pregnant every second of every day; it is an internal experience. But a partner can only think about the pregnancy, he cannot live it: it can only be an external experience. Adjustment cannot help but happen at a different pace. And the schism is immediate, even if on the surface both partners appear to be responding identically.[26].

And Jane Price says in *Motherhood: What It Does to Your Mind:* 'It is therefore easily possible for a couple who were at a similar point of maturity nine months earlier, with so much in common, to reach delivery already far apart.'[27]

For both prospective parents the arrival of children is a major milestone, but it is the woman's life which is transformed beyond recognition. She goes into hospital pregnant and comes out a different person with a different life ahead; he collects a different person from hospital and then goes back to his old job and his old routine. So most women have two or even three lives: Before Children, With Children and After Children have left home. Men's lives traditionally have been divided differently: full-time education, work and retirement.

Becoming a Mother

> ❮ *Well, obviously I had to think about this little person much more than myself. And I think it made me a nicer person because I was thirty-four then and after thirty-four we can become quite selfish. But suddenly there is someone that you love more than anyone else, more than yourself. This child needs you. Whether you've got a child of six months or sixteen years or thirty, you're a mother for life.'* ❯
>
> Barbara is in her early 40s and lives with her husband and 7-year-old son in Hertfordshire.

Throughout recent history mothers have been viewed as kind, caring, giving sorts of people. Mothers are supposed to be patient and uncomplaining and always in tune with their children. They are always supposed to put the needs of others before their own. For example, Kowarzik and Popay, in their report *That's Women's Work*, argue that in the early decades of the twentieth century responsibility for a child's entire wellbeing was laid at the mother's door. And, even though they note the current wide acceptance that others, notably fathers, have a contribution to make, the dominant ideology remains one that places the prime responsibility for [emotional development] with the mother'.[28]

Having a baby – especially for women who have had little contact with small children – is like taking on a new job with few guidelines. For many mothers the first months at home with a new baby are characterised by a sense of loss: loss of identity, loss of adult company and loss of income. She loves her child, but she feels lonely and helpless. She has been living her life in the outside world, and suddenly she has to retreat into a private world. Perhaps for the first time since her own childhood she is dependent.

Even getting themselves and the baby dressed by tea-time, and struggling to complete domestic tasks and deal with a crying baby at the same time can be an overwhelming challenge. Motherhood is often a case of relearning how to do even the most basic jobs; the woman is haunted by the possibility of getting it wrong and the guilt at not having done it well enough. These day-to-day tasks can be fulfilling, but often they are frustrating, particularly if the husband does not understand the nature of the challenge. Later, the challenges change, but the anxieties go on. Three-year-olds are unlikely to die in their sleep from cot death, but they can inflict severe stress on their parents with their anti-social behaviour in public places or their refusal to accept a new brother or sister. Motherhood involves not just caring and giving but also mediating, negotiating, cajoling, setting acceptable boundaries, taking reasonable risks and so on. Motherhood also means overall responsibility for the organisation and care of children and home. A Gallup survey for Farley's baby food manufacturers, conducted in July 1992, showed that 50 per cent of husbands sometimes feed and change the baby; one in three will bath the baby; but one in four refuse to do housework or shopping and one in five never help at all!

Even when both partners work, it is the woman who carries the responsibility of looking after the house and caring for the children. Working women average three hours a day housework, working men seventeen minutes;

working mothers spend an average of fifty minutes a day exclusively with their children, working fathers twelve minutes. Husbands watch TV on average an hour longer than their working wives and sleep half an hour longer each night.[29]

Men's role in caring for their children, in fact, contrasts sharply with what people think ought to happen: 51 per cent of those questioned thought the task of looking after sick children ought to be shared equally between men and women, compared with the 30 per cent who reported that they did share it equally; 67 per cent reported that it was done mainly by the mother. On the question of 'teaching children discipline', 82 per cent said it should be shared equally. In fact, only 67 per cent reported that it was; 19 per cent said it was done mainly by women and 13 per cent mainly by men.

> *It's a lot harder on Mum, it really is. My husband wouldn't agree, although he has come a long way from the man I married. Unless he actually did the Mum role, fitting in the extras and running here and there and taking them to the swimming lessons and the maths tutor and down to Cubs and back again and collecting them from the station, he wouldn't appreciate it. He says, 'Well, I go to work every day and I'm tired.' But I do think it's easier to be at work and I don't think Dads appreciate that. They think it's awfully easy, but it isn't.*
>
> Janine is in her early 30s with two sons. She works part-time and lives with her husband in Surrey.

The gap between opinion and practice is as wide over the question of household chores. For example, 45 per cent said that the task of preparing the evening meal should be shared equally, yet only 17 per cent reported that it was; 77 per cent reported that it was done mainly by women. While 54 per cent said cleaning should be shared equally, only 23 per cent reported that it was; 72 per cent reported that it was done mainly by the

woman.[30] But the 1980s and early 1990s have seen a slight
increase in the numbers of men taking part in household
tasks; so, as Anna Coote and Patricia Hewitt point out,
'. . . we can perhaps anticipate a narrowing of the gap between expectation and reality in the coming decades'.[31]

Witherspoon and Prior, writing in the fifth British
Social Attitudes report, found that part-time working
women have the worst of both worlds, since it is clearly
part of what they call 'the bargain' in these households
that men do very little housework. Their research also
shows that, although the majority view is that 'men
should help out more', in practice most men were making
few efforts to do so and many women also felt that it was
their job to care for the home alone. Witherspoon and
Prior also conclude that these jobs constitute a large part
of the service work within the household and are likely to
place limits on a woman's availability for paid employment.[32]

A report from the Policy Studies Institute in 1989
attempted to understand why women continued to
assume domestic responsibility even when they were
working the same hours as their husbands and, in some
cases, earning more. The report concludes:

> Pervasive among the women was the assumption that
> mothers, but not fathers, can choose whether or not to
> undertake paid employment. This assumption was re-
> inforced by the widespread belief that, for mothers, children
> and family come first and, therefore, mothers should be will-
> ing to give up their paid work if their children suffered from
> their absence . . . Domestic work and children, they believe,
> are their responsibility; paid work is their choice.[33]

The report also cites a study of thirty families where the
wife was employed in a profession and the husband as a
manual worker. With the wife's income exceeding that of
the husband, it might be expected that different domestic
arrangements would prevail. In fact, although the study
did uncover a few families where domestic responsibility
was shared, it concluded that in the majority of families
the woman continued to do both, adding: 'Many wives

still carry the double burden so common in women's lives'.[34]

A study of couples with young children, conducted by Kathryn Backett over a period of fifteen months, shows that mothers are seen as being more readily available than fathers to the child. So, mothers consider themselves to be in the front line when it comes to illness or other occasions when a parent needs to take time off work. A mother believes her absences have a profound impact on the family, but views her partner's absences as an inevitable part of fatherhood.[35]

Becoming a Father

A 1992 Gallup survey jointly sponsored by the Working Mothers' Association and BhS (British Home Stores) concluded that the qualities a parent most needs are 'the stamina of a long distance runner combined with an un-flappable approach to life'. Next on the women's list of priorities was 'having a partner who not only knows where to buy bleach but also how to apply it down the toilet'.[36]

Couples often describe their marriage as a partnership, although this is not yet reflected in the way responsibilities are distributed within most families. As one contributor to Sean French's recent book *Becoming a Father* wisely comments: 'Becoming a father, that is no achievement. Being one, that is'.[37] Sadly, not all men see it like that.

This pattern is reinforced by the amount of time that each partner spends at home. Two separate studies conducted by the Thomas Coram Research Foundation in 1983 and 1986 showed that only 8 per cent of fathers took more than two weeks off work after the birth of their first child. Half had a week or less. Women who returned to work after the birth took an average of 14 weeks' leave.[38] Fathers still have no right in law to take time off work after the birth of a child. There is still no statutory provision for paternity leave in the UK – unlike Germany, for example, which offers 12 months (at a low, flat-rate payment) and Sweden, where fathers have nine months' paid leave at 90 per cent of their salary followed by three months at a flat rate.[39]

To compensate for the drop in family income when the mother stops working, men with dependent children often spend more hours at work than men without children: the reverse is true for women. When children were 18-months-old, 21 per cent of fathers worked between sixty to sixty-nine hours, while 11 per cent worked seventy hours or more.[40] Apart from paid overtime, men with children, especially those in manual and semi-skilled jobs are also more likely to take on shift work or seek out a second job.

> *He never took any responsibility for the children. Financially, he provided us with a wonderful home, everything we needed, but he would never change the nappies. Well, he did it once with my third baby and he was sick halfway through. He said, 'There's no way I can do this', and he never changed another nappy. When they cried he'd say, 'The baby's crying' or 'You go and see to it – I don't want to.'*
>
> Shelly, 35, lives in Portsmouth. Divorced with three children she works in a supermarket.

Kathryn Backett's study, cited earlier, demonstrates the impact that such long hours can have on the way families are organised. Although the couples she interviewed saw the relationship between a father and his child as the most important aspect of fatherhood, time and other pressures meant that this was the area where fathers have least involvement. Fathers, she suggests, are expected to be directly involved with their children and to take an active interest, but not to participate fully and constantly. Many fathers want to watch their children's sports day alongside their wives, and make efforts to do so. But others do not involve themselves in these activities at all.

Mothers have greater knowledge of the child and his or her needs because of their day-to-day involvement. So the mother is usually the father's main source of information about the children. The role of the father is concentrated into two broad areas. First, he acts as second-in-command to support his partner with her childrearing activities. He shares practical and psychological pressures when both partners are present, and deputises in her absence.

Second, he is kept informed about domestic matters such as finance, maintenance of the home, decisions about education, organisation of family leisure time and so on. Fathers' involvement at this level, however, is usually passive – just receiving information from their wives. Domestic matters, especially concerning the children, seem to constitute a major part of everyday conversation.[41]

> *It worries me, I must admit. I went to do some late-night shopping one night when my son was about nine months old, and when I got back – I'd only been gone about half an hour – it was pandemonium. He had practically climbed the walls, the tot was crying, he couldn't find him any juice although I'd left juice for him. It was total panic.*
>
> Liz is 32 and has two children. Her husband is an electrician and they live in London.

Feminists have been accused of reinforcing this pattern of fatherhood by arguing that men have no contribution to make to the family unit. Writing in the *Guardian* in September 1992, Suzanne Moore said: 'Having a father helps kids stop being poor, educationally retarded and delinquent. Apart from that, though, it remains unclear what fathers do that is so damn important.'[42] Men's role in the family *should* be more important than it is, but it remains a dramatically more remote one than that of the mother.

Mothers have taken on childcare responsibilities single-handed. Many women, particularly those who are not in paid employment and therefore have lives based around their home and children, want to ensure that they are the single most important adult in their children's life. They do not want to relinquish any part of that role, even to their husbands, and so guard their special relationship even when circumstances mean that it would be more sensible to accept help.

In those cases fathers are rarely left in charge and most lack experience of looking after children by themselves. Attempts by fathers to take on more responsibility for children can end in failure – deliberate, sometimes – leaving women with the view that it's easier to do it themselves. This reinforces men's helplessness in caring for their children, and so they leave women to get on with it.

Even though there are risks involved, men will not participate in the care of their children if they feel that their efforts do not measure up to the exacting standards of their partner. They will not learn if they are not allowed to make mistakes. Equally, they must realise that simply earning the money and reading a bedtime story once a week is not enough fathering. The more men put into their children, the more everyone will get out of family life: men, women and their children.

Family Pressures

Having children means coping with new and sudden pressures, and both partners can be sorely tested as they try to face up to parenthood. As the NSPCC acknowledges: 'Children of all ages require an enormous amount of their parents' energy and patience – sometimes more than you feel able to give. You have your own needs to take care of as well. At times it can be hard to balance the two.'[43] If partners are sharing the pressures, then the level of stress and frustration will be less damaging than if the mother carries the load alone. The enjoyment and fulfilment will be the greater, too, when families share things.

> ❛*I think both of us became more aware that there was another person in our lives, which we both loved. But at the same time we didn't balance it out enough. I felt that I put too much into the baby and not enough into him. His attitude was 'I've got to work late tonight because the baby's first Christmas is coming and we've got to buy the baby this or that.' But then the pressure would get on top of him and he would need to get out of the house. We became strangers, we never sat down and talked like we used to do, we never shared each other's experiences.*❜
>
> Tracey, 35 and divorced, lives in Worthing. A trained hairdresser, she now fills shelves in a super-market.

Alongside the difficulty of coming to terms with change itself, newly formed families face other pressures. In particular, financial problems increase when children are born and so do the pressures on time: time as a couple, time for yourself, time for sleep. Partners find themselves cast adrift from one another. At a time when each partner needs maximum support, many find themselves heading in different directions – she towards playgroups and part-time employment, he to support the family and sustain his career.

Children, Time and Money

> ❛*Basically, it was down to me, full stop. I don't think it really changed his life at all. On the other hand, he earned more money than me. That was certainly a factor. He paid the mortgage and bills. At the time it didn't bother me that much, but looking back on it I still think I got the rough end of the stick.*❜
>
> Ruth is a solicitor. She has a 12 year old daughter and lives with her second husband in Kent.

Nowadays, the woman makes an important contribution to a family's finances. Her pay has usually been taken into account for the calculation on the mortgage, and is part of the monthly budget. So deciding to have a child has immediate consequences for the family's finances.

For some families it seems difficult for either partner to give up work. For others, the cost of childcare – especially where there is more than one child – outweighs the benefit of two salaries. Women earn on average 71.1 per cent of what men earn.[44] When it comes to deciding who earns and who cares, there is often no contest. The family could not live on her pay alone, so it makes sense for the woman to stay home with the children.

In a report published in 1990, Heather Joshi calculated the financial effects of motherhood on a woman's earnings. Her analysis shows that a 'typical' mother of two earns £163,000 between the ages of seventeen and sixty. A woman without children would earn £285,000 over the same period. The difference is £122,000: Joshi describes this as the 'cash opportunity cost of childbearing'.[45]

Most women do not, of course, see motherhood as a lost 'cash opportunity'. Bringing up the next generation is a privilege, not something to be weighed against the cost in hard cash. But struggling to make ends meet is a undoubtedly further pressure on family life. The current recession has had a devastating impact on families. When the family income plunges, it hits families with small children particularly hard. The following advice from the NSPCC may be sound, but it is of little comfort to parents who have fallen six months behind with the mortgage payments: 'If you're worried about money or you're unhappy with where you live, life can be very stressful indeed . . . Remember that your child's greatest need is love, and that children who are loved and respected will usually grow into well-balanced adults, whatever the circumstances.'[46]

If being a parent is financially demanding, it is also exhausting due to weariness and lack of sleep. In her book *The Second Shift*, Arlie Hochschild describes women 'who talked about sleep the way a hungry person would talk about food'.[47]

Being a parent in paid employment is even more exhausting, because time for the children has to be compressed into smaller spaces. Many parents compensate for their absences by talking about 'quality time' with their children. The concept of arriving home, refreshed by a stimulating day in the office, obviously has some foundation in reality, especially when the children are older and can stay up later to share their own day in an adult way. But it can be very stressful, and a more realistic picture is of exhausted parents struggling home after a difficult day at work and trying unsuccessfully to shift gear between their work life and their children. Fathers tend to develop strategies for handling this situation, such as arriving home after the children are in bed, business trips, breakfast meetings and going to the pub after work.[48]

Sylvia Ann Hewlett, the American Author of *When the Bough Breaks*, is contemptuous of the concept of 'quality time'. She argues that stress-filled working days compromise people's ability to be parents. She also contrasts the characteristics needed to care for children with the very different, assertive personality required to be successful in the labour market. Under 'Qualities Needed to Succeed in Chosen Career' she lists drive for high performance. Under 'Qualities Needed to Meet Needs of Child' she includes time together as a family, stability, a tolerance of chaos, an ability to let go, an acceptance of difference and failure, and an ability to tie the same pair of shoelaces twenty-nine times with patience and humour.[49]

The way that working mothers fit housework and children into an overcrowded evening, juggling chores as they deal with the children, is accurately described by Hochschild. 'If you have ever tried to combine these tasks you will know how frustrated a three- or nine-year-old can become dealing with and depending on half the attention of a weary, irritable mother.'[50]

So, having children can mean shortage of time for the children, shortage of time for yourself and shortage of time for your partner. Husbands and wives working together will overcome these problems; other kinds of marriage will suffer, and the relationships between parents and their children will be unsatisfactory. The century gap is therefore summed up by the family where Mum shops in her lunch hour, collects the children from the minder, cooks tea, puts them to bed, then makes mental notes for the next morning while clearing up the toys and loading the washing machine. Dad rings from the pub to say goodnight to the children ...

This kind of life is very stressful for women. It is not uncommon to hear of mothers who give up work their paid job because there is so little help or support with the unpaid work of bringing up children and running a home. At the same time, fathers are missing out on their children. There is clearly a need to see the early years of parenting as a time when both partners can defer ambition and focus on their family without jeopardising their incomes or their future careers. This cannot be achieved without action by Government and employers to narrow the century gap at this crucial stage in family life.

Children in the Crossfire

> ❛My eldest boy, he doesn't have contact with his father. He feels very hurt by him because there was a lot of violence which he was in the middle of. The younger boy, he uses him. His attitude is when I've got no money and I need some extra money and Mum won't give it to me, I'll go round and see Dad. The little girl, she's only six, so at the moment Dad is someone who buys her sweets, takes her to places I can't afford to take her ... so I let her carry on.❜
>
> Michelle, 36, is divorced and lives in Southampton. She has three children and works as a dinner lady.

It is the children who will always be most vulnerable to changes and upheavals in family life, and therefore the children who are most likely to be the victims of century-gap tension. Children who lose contact with their fathers lose out. Children whose mothers remain a lone parent lose out financially. And children whose mothers remarry may benefit financially but may suffer relationship difficulties when they grow up.

It is the fear of less income that makes so many men spend such a large amount of their time working. In 1993 it has been estimated that, of the 9 million people currently considered to be living in poverty in Britain, as many as 1.25 million are dependent children. All statistics show that children who live in better-off families are less likely than those from poor families to experience difficulties as they grow up.[51]

Family size can be a deciding factor when income is reduced. This is one area where family size and expectation differ between the different ethnic groups which make up British society. Compared with either white or Afro-Caribbean families, Indian, Pakistani and Bangladeshi groups tend to have larger households and larger families per household. The mean number of dependent children where the family head is Indian is 2.1, 2.9 when Pakistani and 3.3 when Bangladeshi: this is compared with 1.8 in families headed by West Indian and white parents and an average of two dependent children per household where the family head is African.

The Asian communities in Britain also tend to have a lower incidence of lone-parent families: between 8 and 9 per cent, compared with 11 per cent of white families, 42 per cent of all West Indian families and 24 per cent of all African families. Afro-Caribbean groups also have more families with a female head: 37 per cent of West Indian families and 20 per cent of African families, compared with 9 per cent of white and 15 per cent of all ethnic families.[52]

Poverty and pressures of the century gap can affect anybody. The role of a woman in a traditional Indian family, for example, is likely to be very different from that of a young middle-class white woman. The difficulties posed by the century gap will be different in each case. Even so, the pressures are affecting every area of society.

The expectations of most people are changing, and those changes will mean that in every class and ethnic group things are no longer being done the way they were.

Becoming a parent does not have to be the cause of problems for today's women and men. Mothers and fathers should be able to enjoy both their working lives and their lives as parents. If the century gap is bridged, then today's children – tomorrow's adults – will be the main winners.

❛We both share looking after him, really. Obviously, if my husband has a day off he takes him to school, takes him to karate or swimming, things like that. Mostly, I take him to school and collect him. Being a Mum means everything really, because we had to wait a long time. If you get married and within three months you're having a baby, then things come easy. But with this child I'm having now we have waited seven years. We were told we probably wouldn't have another one, then suddenly out-of-the-blue I found I was pregnant again. I couldn't believe it until I saw the scan, and it means everything.❜

Sheila, 41, has one son and lives in London with her husband, a welder.

Notes

1. Oakley, A., *Housewife* (Allen Lane, London, 1974)
2. Rapoport, R. and Rapoport, R., 'Work and Family in Contemporary Society' in Edwards, J., *The Family and Change* (Knopf, New York, 1969)
3. OPCS Demographic Review, 1977
4. British Social Trends Since 1900
5. Oakley, A., op. cit.
6. Lundberg, F. and Farnham, M., *Modern Woman: The Lost Sex* (Harper & Bros, New York, 1947)
7. Bowlby, J., '44 Juvenile Thieves: Their Characters and Home Life' in *International Journal of Psychology, Vol. xxv*, 1944
8. Price, J., *Motherhood: What It Does to Your Mind* (Pandora, London, 1988)
9. General Household Survey 1992
10. *Good Housekeeping*, November 1992

11. Mosse, J., op. cit.
12. *Options*, November 1992
13. OPCS Population Trends 1991
14. Faludi, S,. op. cit.
15. Witherspoon, S. and Prior, G., 'Working Mothers: Free to Choose?' in British Social Attitudes Survey 1991/2
16. Coote, A., Harman, H. and Hewitt, P. 'The Family Way', IPPR Social Policy Paper No. 1 1990
17. General Household Survey 1990
18. Land, H. in Gieve, J. (ed.), *Balancing Acts* (Virago, London, 1989)
19. *Guardian*, 7 March 1991
20. Kennedy, H., in *Balancing Acts*, op. cit.
21. OPCS Population Trends Winter 1992
22. *Good Housekeeping*, February 1992
23. Campbell, Beatrix, *Wigan Pier Revisited* (Virago, London, 1984)
24. Roberts, Y., *Mad About Women, Can There Ever Be Fair Play Between the Sexes?* (Virago, London, 1992)
25. Clulow, C., *To Have and to Hold* (Aberdeen University Press, Aberdeen, 1982)
26. Mosse, K., op. cit.
27. Price, J., op. cit.
28. Kowarzik, and Popay, 'That's Women's Work', Employment and Training Group of the London Research Centre, April 1989
29. Hewlett, S., *When the Bough Breaks: The Cost of Neglecting our Children* (Basic Books, 1991)
30. Social Trends 1990
31. Coote, A., Harman, H. and Hewitt, P., op. cit.
32. Witherspoon, S. and Prior G., op. cit.
33. Macrae, S., 'Flexible Working Time and Family Life: A Review of Changes' (Policy Studies Institute, London, 1989)
34. Macrae, S., op. cit.
35. Backett, K., in *Reassessing Fatherhood* Lewis, C. and O'Brien, M. (eds), (Sage Publications, 1987)
36. Working Mothers' Association, March 1992
37. French, S., *Becoming a Father* (Virago, London, 1992)
38. Moss, P., and Brannen, J., in *Reassessing Fatherhood*, op. cit.
39. Moss, P., and Brannen, J., op. cit.
40. Moss, P., and Brannen, J., op. cit.
41. Backett, K., op. cit.
42. *Guardian*, 17 September 1992
43. *Stress: A Guide for Parents*, NSPCC 1992
44. New Earnings Survey 1992
45. Joshi, H., in *Population Studies, 44, 1990*
46. NSPCC, op. cit.
47. Hochschild, A., op. cit.
48. Price, J., op. cit.
49. Hewlett, S., op. cit.
50. Hochschild, A., op. cit.
51. Coote, A., Harman, H. and Hewitt, P., op. cit.
52. OPCS Population Trends Autumn 1989

Chapter 6

Childcare for the Twenty-first Century

❝ With ideal childcare I think I probably would have stayed on at work – I wouldn't have had to give up my job. I worked up to having my second child, but then by the time I got pregnant for the third it was too difficult and I was paying childminders too much. By the time you added up how much you have to pay the childminder and the train fares we weren't really making anything. ❞

Deidre is in the final year of a psychology degree. She has three children and lives in London.

When women are at work, someone else needs to care for their children. But despite the growing number of women at work and the economic importance of women's work both to their family and to the country as a whole, the care of working mothers' children is seen as a private matter for the mother to arrange and pay for. Childcare is not seen as a responsibility to be shared by society – even though we need women's work and we all have a vested interest in the next generation. It is not seen as a responsibility to be shared by men – even though they are their children too.

Childcare is caught in the century gap. For most working women childcare is a headache. There are not enough nursery places, there are not enough childminders. The cost is a hidden tax on working women and prevents some mothers from working at all. It locks them into a poverty trap where they are better off on benefits than if they work and pay for childcare, as the excellent report

Childcare in a Modern Welfare System points out: 'It [childcare] has a vital role to play not only in meeting children's needs, but also in enabling adults to combine the responsibilities of parenthood with paid employment.'[1]

In the past, the nation's need for women to work, such as in wartime, prompted the Government to provide childcare. Now, even though women's work is still necessary to the British economy, the childcare that should underpin it is simply not there. Childcare needs to move into the twenty-first century, and Britain must catch up with other European countries; it is not acceptable that Britain's children are the poor relations of Europe.

Indeed, the development of childcare in this country could be characterised as one step forward and two steps back.

In 1816 the founder of the Co-operative Movement, Robert Owen, opened a nursery for his employees' children in the mill town of New Lanark in Scotland. The nursery was to be a play area for children 'from the time they walk alone until they enter school' and was a demonstration of Owen's own progressive educational theories. Children between the ages of five and ten could also congregate there before and after school. He knew that this would be of benefit not only to the children:

> ... the parents will be relieved from the loss of time and from the care and anxiety which are now occasioned by attendance on their children. The child will be placed in a situation of safety, where with its future school fellows and companions it will acquire the best habits and principles, while at meal times and at night it will return to the caresses of its parents and the affections of each are likely to be increased by the separation.[2]

In Owen's Institute, the functions of care and education were linked and integral to the extensive welfare programme developed for his employees. Care and education of young children would later develop into separate disciplines, but the dual emphasis of what has now become known as 'educare' was not uncommon during the first half of the 19th century. In Germany and Belgium voluntary organisations were developing provision for working-class families along the same lines.

The first public involvement with childcare in the UK was triggered by the First World War, when women were needed to do the jobs vacated by men who had gone to the trenches, and over a hundred day nurseries were set up throughout the country. At the end of the war, local health authorities were empowered by law to provide day nurseries or to assist voluntary (private) nurseries. Schools established under the 1870 Education Act took in a considerable number of children of the two-to-five age group, and by 1901 43 per cent of three-year-olds in England and Wales were on elementary school registers.[3]

The 1918 Education Act allowed local authorities to establish nursery schools themselves, but they were slow to take up this option. By 1938 there were only 4,000 places in public nurseries and just over 9,500 in nursery education. But the Second World War once again prompted an increase in provision, and by 1945 there were nursery places for 62,000 children in England and Wales, with similar programmes in Scotland and Northern Ireland.

However, as the view that women should stay at home and raise their young children took hold, nurseries began to close again; by 1965 only a third remained open. During this same period, the number of places with registered childminders increased from 1,700 to 47,200. The need for childcare remained, but once children were seen as the mother's responsibility, family issues such as childcare were excluded from the scope of welfare reform. Despite the fact that women with children did work, this was seen as an undesirable state of affairs and this view was reflected in the lack of public nursery provision. A Ministry of Health circular in 1968 recommended that priority for nursery places should be given to children with only one parent 'who has no option but to go out to work', or to those with health or welfare needs.

Who Minds the Children?

Childcare in Britain today reflects the work patterns and ideals of thirty years ago, and fails to meet the needs of society as it now is. Since 43 per cent of women with young children go out to work, 13 per cent of them full-time, the organisation and financing of childcare is of greater importance than it was even in the early 1980s, when only 29 per cent of women with pre-school children worked, and only 6 per cent full-time.

Most people still see it as the woman's rather than the man's responsibility to arrange childcare, even if both are working. Parents want to be satisfied that their children are being properly looked after. Finding a job that fits in with school hours is the solution sought by many women: but few jobs are tailored to the 8.45 to 3.30 day, or cease during school holidays and half-terms.

‘I would like to go back to being a telephonist, but it would mean me having someone to take them to school and also some-one to pick them up and have them until the time I came home. And, of course, you've got the school holidays, which is a major bind. So at the moment I do house cleaning and just have the holidays off.’

Frances, 37, is divorced and lives in Hertfordshire with her three children.

The kind of childcare people use depends to some extent on the age of their children. Of women with children aged five to eleven, 16 per cent ask a friend or neighbour to help out, compared with 1 per cent of mothers of under-fives.[5] The most recent figures available reveal that state-registered nurseries in the UK only cater for between 2 and 3 per cent of the total under-five population. In the 1991 General Household Survey, 21 per cent of parents with pre-school children said they used nurseries; 20 per cent used unpaid family and friends; 14 per cent a private or voluntary scheme; 9 per cent a paid childminder or nanny; 6 per cent a local authority scheme; and 1 per cent a workplace nursery.[6]

Women with children between five and eleven often have different systems for termtime and school holidays. In the survey, 23 per cent used unpaid family and friends during the holidays, with 18 per cent keeping to that arrangement during termtime too; 7 per cent had a paid childminder or nanny; 2 per cent used a private or voluntary scheme; 2 per cent used a local authority scheme during the holidays, with half of those mothers using them during termtime as well; and 1 per cent used a workplace nursery.[7]

The stark revelation is the degree to which mothers – and fathers – have to rely on the goodwill of their family and friends to look after their children. Before adequate solutions can be found to the difficulties posed by the century gap in childcare, it is essential that the true extent of the unmet need is recognised.

> *The cost of childcare is horrendous – and because women are not paid as highly it is a terrific strain. It does make you wonder if it is worth it.*
>
> Laura, 42, is divorced and lives in Fife with her daughter. She is a full-time secretary and works evenings too.

One of the most comprehensive surveys of childcare was conducted by the Scottish Low Pay Unit in 1992. In interviews with more than 3,500 people, they found that a third used formal childcare services such as childminders or nurseries, but two-thirds relied on informal arrangements. Costs of childcare are usually borne by the woman, since working is seen as a choice rather than a necessity. Mothers interviewed paid, on average, between £10 and £60 a week, and the majority of those interviewed said that childcare costs represented 10–50 per cent of their take-home pay. A few said that it amounted to more than half.[8]

Childcare is segregated by social class and income. Those who can afford a live-in nanny – which can cost anything up to £300 per week, when salary, national insurance contributions and board and lodging are taken into account – have greater flexibility and choice than those who cannot afford to pay at all and must rely on the availability of local authority nursery places. Researchers from the Thomas Coram Institute state that public day-care services have a heavy concentration of children from disadvantaged backgrounds, because many councils allocate scarce places on the basis of need. Playgroups, on the other hand, are used disproportionately by middle-class children. Do we, they ask, 'want to encourage the development of a separate system of services for children with employed parents?'[9]

Full-time private nurseries can cost from £50 to £150 per week. The social and ethnic mix of children will depend on the community which the nursery is serving and the fees charged. Nursery provision tends to be more widespread in the major cities. Some nurseries operate all year round, while others follow standard school terms. Few nurseries accept children under the age of two, and others take children under four only on a part-time basis.

Some local authorities have made great efforts to provide or co-ordinate childcare services. For example, North Tyneside Council co-ordinates a range of services through a Childcare Shop. Parents explain their requirements and are then directed to the relevant kind of care. The scheme is seen as an essential component of the local authority's strategy for aiding economic development and regeneration. In Scotland, Fife Regional Council is developing a Partnership in Childcare schemes; while in West London the Borough of Hammersmith and Fulham has developed a pilot project combining out-of-school play facilities with a care service for children aged five to twelve. Manchester City Council has opened six children's centres, and has plans for six more. But nowhere in the UK does the availability of nursery places begin to meet the demand.

Because there is such a high demand for so few nursery places, some councils, as mentioned above, allocate places on the basis of need. The children who qualify are those in danger of being taken into care, those on the 'at risk' register, or those whose families are beset with problems. Once attained, that nursery place is subject to periodic review: if the mother's circumstances improve, her child can lose its place in favour of another child in worse home circumstances.

This system of allocation ensures that in certain areas all the children in nurseries have multiple problems, thus reinforcing their disadvantage; the mere fact of attending such a nursery on this basis can stigmatise a child. The review system encourages the mother to emphasise her failure to cope, in case any signs of improvement in her life result in the loss of the much-needed nursery place. This situation is very far from how things would be if nursery places were more widely available; then children from families with problems would benefit because they could share nurseries with children of mothers who need a nursery place simply because they go out to work.

> *My wife was nursing ... it was the only way we could cope. By the time I was coming home from work it was 7 and she was going off at 7.30 in the evening to start work. She was getting home at 6 in the morning and I was going off at 6.30, so sometimes we would only see each other for an hour a day. It was the only way we could make it financially viable. That way there was always somebody around to look after the children and we didn't have to pay a childminder. We never had a childminder at all. That was the only way we could cope.*
>
> Martin is in his 40s with two children. His wife is a nurse and they live in Plymouth.

The most common form of childcare outside the family is a childminder. Under the terms of the 1989 Children Act no one can charge a fee for looking after a child in their own home unless they are registered with a local authority. Pressure on council resources means it can take months for the local authority to complete the registration procedure, leading to a backlog of those who want to work as childminders but who are as yet unable to take on any children. Even so, registered childminders are now used by 14 per cent of women with children under twelve.

As with nannies and nurseries, the quality of child-minders varies enormously. A childminder's home is checked to see if it is safe for children, and police files are scrutinised to see if either the childminder or her husband has a criminal record that would be incompatible with the care of children. No formal qualifications are required: childminders are usually young mothers with children with families of their own, who want to earn a little extra money.

Rates vary hugely from one area to another, but broadly speaking it costs between £40 and £90 a week to send a child to a childminder. Food is sometimes included, and sometimes mothers have to provide it. There is a limit on the number of children a woman can care for, which includes her own – it ranges from three to six – and there cannot be more than one child under the age of eighteen months. Good childminders may also belong to playgroups and other schemes; but some simply leave the children watching television all day.

❝I remember one particular childminder who looked after my son. My son has always been very greedy so I would send lots of food for him and he loved yogurt, so I always ensured I sent his yogurt. One day I went there and I didn't tell her I was coming. I got there and her son was eating my son's yogurt. She said to me: 'Oh, he didn't want it' and I knew that was a blatant lie because I know he would never, ever refuse yoghurt.❞

Erica is 38 and lives in London with her husband and four children. She used to work in telephone sales.

Britain's Children: Europe's poor Relations

In most other European countries childcare for the under threes is offered through a mix of individual and group arrangements. Provision for children over three is based around a core nursery or kindergarten system. Evidence published in an authoritative and far-reaching Equal Opportunities Commission Report[10] reveals that

95 per cent of all French children between the ages of three and six go to *école maternelle* (nursery school), which is free and provided by the Ministry of Education. About a third of two-year-olds also attend these schools, and there are a wide variety of full-day services for other children under three, including community nurseries and some workplace nurseries (the majority of which are in hospitals).[11]

In all other countries in the European Community except Britain and Portugal, the majority of children over three have places in publicly funded childcare services: 95 per cent in Belgium, 85 per cent in Italy, 70 per cent in Spain, Greece and Germany. In Britain, the absence of any national childcare policy means that most parents have to rely on what they can afford, unless they happen to live somewhere where the council provides free nurseries for after-school schemes.[12]

❛ *When I was doing part-time work my only choice was to take the children with me. It would have been a lot easier if there had been some kind of childcare available. Maybe a creche, where you could take them for the hours you worked and you knew they would be looked after and safe and cared for. I think there might be more available nowadays, but fifteen years ago there weren't.* ❜

Trudi, 35, lives in Brighton with her three children. She is working as a cleaner while she retrains in computers.

A 1990 survey for the *Daily Telegraph* found that 88 per cent of people asked thought the Government should increase the availability of childcare for working women, and 87 per cent also thought that the Government should provide more nursery education.[13] Yet public spending on childcare has hardly increased over the past ten years, despite the revolution in the numbers of women working.

Many women feel they cannot work at all because of lack of satisfactory childcare. A survey in 1979 looked at the reasons women gave for not returning to work after the birth of a child: 35 per cent cited lack of childcare provision or its cost, while a further 26 per cent said that the lack of a job with suitable hours made working out of the question.[14]

For most working women childcare is either too expensive, of too poor quality, too unreliable or not available at all. Where there is good-quality, affordable childcare the mother's peace of mind is so dependent on it they feel it is too good to be true, and fear it will collapse: the nursery will close, the grandparent will fall ill, the childminder will move to a different part of the city.

Once a child is at school the problems change, but do not vanish. Most school hours are 9–3.30 for primary and 9–4 for secondary. In state schools, each term is roughly fourteen weeks long, divided by half-terms of one week. Beyond this, education authorities in different parts of the country organise their timetables in all sorts of way. The school holidays account for about eight weeks of the year and school weeks are now punctuated by 'inset' days when there is no school for the children because the teachers are involved in in-service training. Of the women interviewed for the 1992 British Social Attitudes Survey, 25 per cent said they only work while their children are at school and 11 per cent (all with children aged five to 11) left their children alone in the house after school until a parent came home.[15]

> 6 *Promotion prospects for women are not as good, because they know that if there's a disaster you're going to rush off home.* 9
>
> Margaret, 42, has three sons and works full-time. She lives in Glasgow.

The Scottish Low Pay Unit survey asked parents to spell out the main problems with their own childcare arrangements. Almost 40 per cent referred to the difficulty of getting time off work to cover illness or school holidays. Indeed, the authors of the report commented that so few parents were able to find work which fitted round the school year that they simply wrote 'school holidays' in answer to the question about problems that they experienced.[16]

Other problems included the cost of childcare, its over-all availability and the difficulty co-ordinating work and childcare. Almost 20 per cent also cited the instability of informal childcare arrangements. Respondents referred to their guilt at encroaching on grandparents' 'well-earned leisure time', and of feeling 'a burden' when they left their child with a relative. One mother said: 'My daughter is looked after by my parents, who are both approaching retirement age. They cope only because they have to, because being a single parent I cannot afford regular full-time childcare.'

The government argues that this situation can be accepted as it represents the operation of a free market; that parental demand is influencing the range of services available. Realistically, as the National Children's Bureau states in the strongest terms, the market cannot provide and so 'parents have little or no choice about the kind of childcare they use.[17]

> 6 *Childcare facilities are not very good. Ideally, I would have liked after-school care when she was older, rather than have a full-time childminder.* 9
>
> Catherine, 40, has one teenage daughter and lives in Carlisle. She works as a secretary.

The case for provision which enables all women and men to fulfil their potential both as parents and as workers has never been stronger. Both women and society suffer when mothers cannot work because of the lack of satisfactory childcare. According to the Equal Opportunities Commission, the long-term consequences of a woman being restricted to lower paid, part-time work after having two children are that a 'typical' break of eight years in total, followed by fourteen years in part-time work, means that her lifetime earnings will only be 57 per cent of those of a woman without children.[18] Not only is the individual family losing out, but society is wasting its human resources. As Joanna Foster, former Chair of the Equal Opportunities Commission, has said: 'The country needs, as at no other time since the Second World War, the skills, energies and ideas of women.'[19]

Research shows that there is a chasm between the kind of childcare women want and what is available to them. As the British Social Attitudes Survey demonstrates, the majority of mothers are strongly committed to caring for children themselves or within the family circle. Of those interviewed, 55 per cent said that in ideal circumstances they work during school hours only, while 58 per cent said that if they needed childcare, a relative would be their first choice.[20] Twenty per cent of women with children under five would prefer workplace nurseries, 14 per cent local council-funded day nurseries and 14 per cent a private nursery. Only 8 per cent mentioned childminders as their choice.

Having my daughter made working a lot more difficult. I had to suddenly start working part-time, working round her. In fact, I gave up being a solicitor altogether and I did secretarial work. I suppose I did that for a couple of years, and when she got to playgroup age started doing legal work again but on a part-time basis. Then the more schooling she had, the more I worked. I finally went back full-time about three years ago when she was nearly nine.

Ruth is a solicitor. She has a 12 year old daughter and lives with her second husband in Kent.

For women with children aged five to 11 the picture was slightly different. Fewer – only 8 per cent – saw a workplace nursery as the answer to out-of-school care; 23 per cent thought they would turn to a friend or neighbour and 10 per cent to a childminder.

Respondents to the Low Pay Unit survey in Scotland were evenly divided on whether the best childcare would be based at home, in the local community, in the workplace or within a school. They were overwhelmingly clear, however, that parents could not go on carrying all the burden of the cost. Almost 70 per cent felt that the cost of childcare should be shared by local authorities, employers and Government as well as parents.[21]

Childcare: The Poverty Trap

The Equal Opportunities Commission's view is that childcare is probably 'one of the most important factors restricting many women's opportunities'.[22] In spite of increasing levels of unemployment, more women with young children than ever before are working outside the home.

An Australian study has shown, however, that the direct cost of purchasing childcare for an individual parent is significantly higher than the income loss incurred by parents who stay at home. In many cases this knowledge alone discourages women from entering the labour market.[23]

The case of Patricia Cresswell highlights the problem. A lone parent with two children, she went to the European Court in May 1992 to expose the poverty trap for women trying to return to paid work after being dependent on benefits. Patricia Cresswell was offered part-time work as a graphic designer. This meant she lost income support and had to pay for childcare: her loss of income support meant she also had to start paying the whole of her mortgage. Her net income when she was employed again was therefore less than it had been when she received state benefits. She lost her case because the European Court of Justice ruled that the UK income support system was not covered by the particular European law in question.

Patricia Cresswell appealed to the Department of Social Security (DSS), arguing that childcare costs should be taken into account when calculating eligibility for income support. This would bring her back into the benefit net and make working financially worthwhile. Her situation is not uncommon.

'Hundreds of thousands of lone parents are trapped on a "poverty plateau" where it makes little difference whether they earn £70 or £170 a week,' ran a *Guardian* article on 17 February 1993 discussing a recent report. 'By the time child care and travel costs are taken into account, any incentive to work may have disappeared, says the report published by the Joseph Rowntree Foundation.' The study states that 'there are 1.3 million lone parents in Britain, nine in ten of them women'.[23a]

> ❛*I had an awful birth first time round, so I stayed off for the full twenty-nine weeks which I don't think pleased anyone. I had less time off with the second one. I do feel I need to work because I'm good at it, and I get that reinforcement and I get the money, too. I suppose I could stop working altogether, but I feel it wouldn't be best for the boys if I was full-time at home because I'm quite short-tempered and quite selfish, although I'm always trying to do the right thing for them. I can't imagine doing lots of painting every day and all the sorts of things that would develop them.*❜
>
> Helen, 35, is a TV journalist. Her husband runs a design company. They have two sons and live in London.

Following up the 1979 maternity rights survey,[24] the 1992 British Social Attitudes Survey has shown that, with better childcare, 30 per cent of part-time working mothers would increase their hours, half of these mothers to full-time. What is more, 65 per cent of women who currently stay at home said that with better childcare they would choose to work. Interestingly, about a quarter of the women who work full-time would reduce their hours if they could.[25]

Research supports the argument that childcare is beneficial, not only in enabling the mother to work, but also in assisting the child's development by enabling him or her to learn and play with other children and to form friendships with adults outside the family. The influential US Ypsilanti study suggests that children with pre-school experience are more likely to complete their

schooling than those who do not; they are more likely to
be employed and are more likely to be able to support
themselves; girls with pre-school experience are less
likely to be teenage mothers, and more likely to have
jobs.[26] Recent British findings are that those children
who attend nursery schools on average adapt better to
primary school than those who have been cared for solely
within the home until the age of five. 'Research has
shown both the immediate and lasting value to the child
of good-quality pre-school experiences, and the benefit to
parents of services that support and enhance their relationship with their children.[27]

Many women who would like to work feel guilty that it
would not be in their child's best interests if he or she
were with a childminder or at a nursery. But if the care is
good, a stimulating environment allows children from all
backgrounds to meet and play together. With proper
childcare provisions women would have more choice in
their place and hours of work.

> *My working life would be so much better if I didn't have to
> race about to pick them up from school. If they could come out of
> school a bit later and have a longer day, that would be fantastic!
> If anything goes wrong, or we're really busy in the pub or my
> hairdressing clients build up, there's a tremendous pressure to get
> back at this particular time which spoils everything. I'm sort of
> on this clock watch all the time.*
>
> Melanie, 35, lives with her husband and two chil-
> dren in Surrey. She used to be an estate agent and now
> works in a pub.

Childcare: the Role of Government

Women's expectations that they will work after having
children, as well as the importance of their work both to
their family's finances and to the economy, now requires
the Government to develop a national childcare policy
which encompasses what is provided, its quality and how

it is paid for. There are strong economic arguments for a national childcare policy. The Institute of Public Policy Research has calculated that public money invested in childcare brings a return. The IPPR cost-benefit analysis demonstrates the savings to the Treasury from 1.8 million additional mothers going out to work. And their model is cautious: it does not, for example, take into account new jobs in childcare, only the reduction in state benefits. If anything, the financial return would be higher than estimated. The IPPR figures suggest that individual families would benefit by between £400 and £3,000 a year; that 1.25 million children currently living in poverty would be brought out of that situation if their mothers worked; and that returns to the Treasury over a thirteen-year period would range from 5 per cent to 51 percent.[28]

The National Children's Bureau has calculated that the cost of a comprehensive state-subsidised system of childcare would raise more taxes than it cost. The NCB estimates that an extra £4 billion in tax revenue would be raised within a decade if subsidised childcare – costing £3.6 billion – were phased in; and that its policy would lift 500,000 children out of poverty.[29]

Providing enough childcare places to allow, say, 1.8 million more women to enter paid work – as the IPPR have suggested – may prove less expensive than many fear, but it is not cost-free. But, however it is accounted, providing care for children always involves some cost: Heather Joshi, for example, makes the point that full-time maternal care imposes heavy long-term costs on individual women who forego earnings and lose pension rights.[30] Society also pays the price through wasted human resources.

It is not, therefore, acceptable for society to assume that women must continue to bear all the invisible costs of childcare fees when they re-enter employment. The role of Government is to recognise the collective benefits to society of childcare and then determine what proportion of costs should be borne by parents, employers and the public purse.

If costs are to be shared, then the Government can

either subsidise services – a supply subsidy – or subsidise parents' costs – a demand subsidy. There are already examples of both systems operating in other countries. In Sweden, day care is funded by a national pay-roll levy and the proceeds are used to provide local services. The United States and some European countries operate systems of tax relief; this is, in effect, a demand subsidy. Among the advantages is that it discourages the 'hidden economy' in childcare, because payments must be declared before they can attract tax relief. But there are disadvantages too, not least that it tends to favour high earners and encourages ad hoc provision rather than the development of a comprehensive service for all. The Netherlands Government abandoned its tax relief system in 1989 because it was not considered successful: the Dutch system had not provided childcare for those who needed it, and had individualised childcare. The result was a return to a publicly funded state system.

Childcare credits and vouchers are another way of subsidising demand. Where tax relief is combined with childcare benefit for parents below the tax threshold, this overcomes the inequity of straightforward tax relief. But tax credits could inflate the cost of childcare and, like tax relief, this proposal makes no direct contribution to a general policy. Arguments over childcare vouchers have also foundered on the problems of whether they should be universally available or given only to those in need.

An interesting scheme, used extensively in Australia and Canada, is fee relief. Childcare services reduce or waive fees on a means-tested basis and are then re-imbursed by the Government. Fee relief may well prove suitable in Britain because it is appropriate in a situation where parents are expected to make some contribution to childcare costs, and where services are intended to be available on an equitable basis. Used in conjunction with other public subsidies in Australia, fee relief has contributed to a significant expansion in childcare places. There were 46,000 available in 1983, but by 1990 the figure had risen to 122,000; estimates are that it will increase to 192,000 by 1994–5.[32]

Debate has also focused recently on what role the state should play in the regulations of nurseries. Traditionally, Government has accepted a role in regulating private nurseries, which have to be registered by the local authority and are refused registration if they do not conform to regulations about such matters as adequate outside play space. Government clearly has a role in checking whether those who set up in business to care for children have criminal records which make them unsuitable. The question of approving premises for fire safety is also important.

But the key role for Government is to make sure that there is a choice of affordable care available to parents. Children are taken to and from nurseries on a daily basis by their parents or another family member or a friend. The parents are in a far better position than the local council to know whether or not a child is happy in the nursery and well cared for. If the child is happy, then the parents are unlikely to take much notice of the council's view of the nursery. Similarly, if the child is unhappy and not thriving, the parents' worries will not be assuaged by being told that the nursery is registered with the council. If parents are dissatisfied and there are other nurseries available in the area, then they will move their child.

The key element in ensuring the quality of nurseries is, therefore, choice. But that choice will not be available unless the Government adopts a national childcare policy which ensures the availability of childcare in all areas. Instead of the emphasis being on extensive regulation over very little provision, it should be on ensuring as wide a provision as possible.

Childcare: the Role of Employers

Employers have a role to play in the development of childcare for the twenty-first century, and organisations such as the Campaign for Tax Relief and Childcare (TRAC) have produced information explaining how companies can best attract high-quality staff by providing help with childcare. In May 1992 TRAC produced a strategy document specifically aimed at extending employer-funded childcare; which stated that 'all forms of legal childcare provision should be exempt from taxation as benefits in kind, where this is paid for or subsidised by the parents' employer'.[33]

> ❝ My wife had every intention of going back to work, because it was a pretty good job and they kept it open. She had six months' maternity leave and she was fortunate to get a job-share, so that helped immensely as far as she was concerned and gave her a bit more time at home. One week she works two days, the next week three days. ❞
>
> Tony, 38, from Birmingham is a manager with British Gas. His wife works for the local council. They have two children.

The most common form of employer-financed childcare programme is the workplace nurseries scheme. Many mothers, particularly those with very young children, have said that their preferred form of provision would be a workplace nursery. This is partly due to a desire to continue breastfeeding, or to the fact that they are on hand in the event of emergency. This kind of provision also means that time and resources do not have to be allocated to dropping off children at a nursery or a childminder's before going on to work. The advantage to the employer is that it creates an incentive for staff to stay. Parents will not want to move their child from the nursery unless absolutely necessary.

However, there are disadvantages too. Travelling to and from work in the rush hour with a young child is often difficult, particularly in big cities. And children may prefer to be involved in local activities rather than far from home. For the parents, the workplace nursery can seriously impair job mobility; some feel that it is more difficult to concentrate on their jobs knowing that their child is close at hand. But there are, as yet, only a small number of workplace nurseries. Fewer than 1 per cent of parents have access to one, and almost all are in the South-east of England.

All forms of employer-provided childcare need to be encouraged, because the unmet need is so great. Many companies now pay childcare allowances to both fathers and mothers, and Scarlett MccGwire's informative book *Best Companies for Women*[34] lists many which offer attractive childcare packages to employees.

The Century Gap Closed

For too long childcare has had too low a priority on the political agenda. And it has only been understood as a welfare issue: allowing women the opportunity to work, and protecting vulnerable children. Part of the century gap will have been bridged when the question of childcare moves from being a welfare issue to being understood also as an economic issue. Childcare will be regarded as an essential component of the economic infrastructure, just as roads, railways and telecommunications now are. If the workforce cannot get to work because there are no roads or railways, the economy is at a disadvantage. Similarly, if half the workforce cannot get to work because of lack of childcare, the economy will suffer. When firms are considering investing in a particular town, they will look not only at the pool of available labour but also at the childcare facilities. And when planning the science parks of the future, childcare centres will be as essential as the roads leading to them.

There should be a national childcare policy, with six guiding principles:

- that childcare is important to the economy
- that it is a key component of a modern welfare systems
- that it must serve a range of interests – parents, children and society
- that provision must be equitable and responsive
- that it must seek to integrate education and care
- that policies must be linked to improved provision for employed parents, such as maternity and paternity leave and access to flexible hours of work.

Notes

1. Cohen, B. and Fraser, for the Institute of Public Policy Research, 'Childcare in a Modern Welfare System', 1991
2. Owen, R., *A New View of Society or Essays on the Principles of Formation of the Human Character and the Application of the Principle to Practice* (Candell & Davies, London, 1813)
3. Summerfield, P., *Women Workers in the Second World War* (Croom Helm, London, 1984)
4. General Household Survey 1991
5. British Social Attitudes Survey 1991–2
6. General Household Survey 1992
7. General Household Survey op. cit.
8. Tait, L., Scottish Low Pay Unit, 1992
9. Thomas Coram Institute, 1992
10. Equal Opportunities Commission, 'The Key to Real Choices: An Action Plan for Childcare', 1990
11. Moss and Melhuish, *Day Care for Young People*, (Routledge, London, 1990)
12. European Commission Childcare Network, December 1990
13. Gallup, 1992
14. Daniels, W., Maternity Rights Survey 1979
15. British Social Attitudes Survey, op. cit.
16. Tait, L., op. cit.
17. National Children's Bureau, 'Working for Childcare', 1991
18. Equal Opportunities Commission Report, 'Parents, Employment Rights and Childcare', December 1992
19. 'The Key to Real Choice', op. cit.
20. British Attitudes Survey, op. cit.
21. Tait, L., op. cit.
22. IPPR 'Childcare in a Modern Welfare System', op. cit.
23. Cass, B., 'Why Public Investment in Childcare Matters: Economic and Social Issues', address presented at Golden Jubilee of Lady Gowrie Child Centre.
23a. *One-parent Families: Policy Options for the 1990s* (Joseph Rowntree Foundation, York, 1993)
24. Daniels, W., op. cit.
25. British Attitudes Survey, op. cit.
26. Osborne, A. and Milbank, J., *The Effects of Early Education: A Report from the Child Health and Education Survey*, (OUP, Oxford, 1987)
27. NCB, op. cit.
28. IPPR, 'Childcare in a Modern Welfare System', op. cit.
29. NCB, op. cit.
30. Joshi, H. and Davies, H., Childcare Institutions in Europe and Mothers' Foregone Earnings, 1991
31. Cass, B., op. cit.
32.
33. TRAC: A Strategy for Employer Funded Childcare, May 1992
34. MccGwire, S., *Best Companies for Women* (Pandora, London, 1992)

Chapter 7

Twenty-first Century Women and Work

> *❛I used to get a lot of stick for leaving my baby. I remember walking through Clapham one day, seeing a girl I used to work with – I was in a different department then. And she thought women going back to work was wrong. Then, three years later, she did exactly the same thing. It's very easy to throw stones at people – very, very easy. Deep down, I felt quite good about working, although on the other hand I didn't like doing it and felt sort of split.❜*
>
> Pat is 40 and lives in London. Married with one son, her husband works as a builder.

The century gap hangs like a dead weight around Britain's economy. Half our college leavers and university graduates are women and by the end of the century half the workforce will be women. Yet the world of work is based on the assumption that all workers are men and that they have a wife at home to look after them and their children. For many people this assumption was never true. But now it is wholly out-of-date.

As capital and raw materials can now be moved around the globe with ease, the economy that will be successful in the future is the one which makes the best use of its people and their skills. It is what are now termed 'human resources' that will give an economy its competitive edge.

We need to recognise that we will see new patterns of works. We must underpin them with new legal rights that reflect the fact that the workforce of today is very different from the workforce of forty years ago. If we continue to work to patterns of the past, we will waste half the talents and energies of our most valuable resources, the workforce of the twenty-first century – men and women.

Women's working lives have already undergone enormous change. Men's working lives are changing too: no longer can they expect to be in the same job all their lives; many face periods of unemployment, and others need to retrain when their original skills are superseded by technology. But the attitudes governing the world of paid employment – the management culture, the legal framework and the social security system – show that it is still structured around how men lived their working lives in the past.

> ❦ *I think for a while I have definitely allowed my career to be a little sidelined. I do get cross when other people who are not as good as me get promoted! I have this sort of dichotomy, knowing that I am not putting as much time into it as I used to, but I am not less committed. I couldn't cut back my hours – it's such a popular profession. Something like 40-odd per cent of all new graduates want to go into the media. We seem to have all these very highly qualified young brains who are so keen to get on and will literally work all the hours God sends and do whatever for nothing.* ❧
>
> Emma is 38 and a radio producer. She has a daughter and lives with her husband in Edinburgh.

At work, women are no longer optional extras, a reserve army of labour to be hired in good times and fired in bad. Women's work is essential to the economy and the family income. Today, although prejudices still exist, working women are slowly breaking down the old male stereotypes of full-time, lifetime work.

The century gap not only divides women from men,

and men from their families, but also women from women. Inside every housewife is a career woman, inside every career woman a housewife – and both are struggling to get out. Whatever decisions women have made about work, many fear that they have made the 'wrong' decision and resent other women who might have made the 'right' one.

The aspiring earth mother and the aspiring career woman will both find plenty of role models in women's magazines. But rather than worrying about the choices that women make, attention should focus on the changes that must be made by employers, managers, trade unions and Government. Only by getting the context right can we stop women's choice being seen as 'wrong'.

The Changing Workforce

The Government's Women and Employment Survey of 1980[1] charted the changes in women's working lives that have taken place this century. Since the Second World War, the proportion of women under retirement age who are in paid work at any one time has steadily risen, increasing by more than 10 per cent in the last ten years alone. The proportion of their lives that women spend in paid employment has also increased: those born in the 1920s spent only half their lives between leaving school and reaching their sixtieth birthday in paid work; those born in the late 1950s can expect to spend two-thirds of their working lives in paid employment. So women now spend most of their working lives employed. Though it varies between different ethnic groups: for Indian, Pakistani and Bangladeshi women domestic and family responsibilities lead to a much lower percentage of time being spent in paid employment.[2]

The Government's projections suggested that population size would continue to increase up until 1981, despite the declining birth rate. Between 1987 and 1995 it is estimated that the number of people aged between sixteen and twenty-four will fall by 30 per cent, that the proportion of

the population between sixteen and sixty-four would remain at around 64 per cent, but that there will be an increase in the number of people aged sixty-five and over.[3]

As a result of demographic trends and changes in economic activity rates, the size of the civilian labour force is
projected to increase by one million up to the turn of the
century. Of that one million increase, 90 per cent will be
women.[4] The Department of Employment forecasts that
this figure will be in the region of 5 million women!

> *I was a secretary/PA, but I have to say I couldn't seem to fit it
> in with being a Mum. I'm doing part-time voluntary work in a
> school at the moment, which I enjoy, and it fits in round my chil-
> dren so I am still there for them.*
>
> Linda is 32 with two children. She lives with her
> husband in Kent.

'Real Work' – Part-time or Full-time

The change in British working patterns is clear when you
look at part-time work. By the year 2000 it is estimated
that 25 per cent of all jobs will be part-time (less than
thirty hours a week)[5], of which the majority will be filled
by women. Eighty per cent of part-time workers throughout the European Community are women, and the number of jobs offering less than sixteen hours' work a week
is growing fast. British women are already more likely to
work part-time than their counterparts in the EC. In
1988, over half of all married women in Britain worked
part-time.[6]

If the century gap between men and women and work
is to be bridged, the value of part-time work must be
recognised. The 1980 Women and Employment Survey
found that one in five employees who worked fewer than
thirty hours a week received no paid holiday, and the
likelihood of their being allowed more than three working

weeks' holiday was considerably less than that of full-time workers. One in three received no sick pay. Women whose working week was under thirty hours and who were returning to work after the birth of their first child were more likely to come back to a lower-paid, lower-status job, and half the women who returned to work on a part-time basis took a drop in seniority – as against one in five of those women who came back for more than thirty hours.[7]

❢ Sometimes I think there are a lot of discrepancies between the part-time and the full-time people at work. The part-timers often think that they are not as good as you. I know when I was in the bank we had two part-time workers. They were both women and they never got to go on any courses or anything like that. They were low-paid – lower-paid than us. They weren't really thought of as proper members of staff. ❢

Nicola is 20 and a university student. She lives with her parents in Reading.

The different levels of protection offered by legislation dealing with unfair dismissal, redundancy pay, statutory sick pay and paid maternity leave are also based on hours of work rather than the value of the work done. Employees working fewer than eight hours per week have almost no rights; those working between eight and fifteen hours wait for a longer qualifying period before they receive certain benefits – five years with the same employer – than those working sixteen hours or more, who usually only need to have been with the company for two years.

The legal rights of part-time workers have been eroded since 1986, when it was estimated that at least half of them were protected by law.[8] And because protection, in most cases, depends on continuous service, employees with term-time and annual contracts may fall outside the law even if they work the requisite number of hours in total.

The idea that only full-time work is real work is no

longer borne out by British working practices. Assumptions are made about what constitutes a real working week, but in fact only one in three British employees now works a standard nine-to-five, five-day week. Working hours for male full-timers have in fact been dropping for more than a century. A series of campaigns by the trade unions succeeded in cutting the working week by a third between 1881 and 1981, and Charles Handy has estimated how the typical male working lifetime for his generation has fallen from approximately a hundred thousand hours (that is, forty-seven hours for forty-seven weeks for forty-seven years). Taking into account shorter hours, longer holidays, more education and earlier retirement, he thinks the figure is now closer to fifty thousand hours. And if the trend towards early retirement continues, the average male working lifetime will drop to around forty years by the turn of the century.[9]

The Importance of Flexibility

> ❲ *Well, we moved to a new house and the boys were all at school and it was terribly quiet. I was really cheesed off, so I saw this job in the paper and thought, 'Right, I'll go for that.' Me and a million others, I thought. I just wrote the letter there and then and posted it and got a call to go for an interview. I thought I might as well go, and I remember by the time I got home off the bus the phone was ringing and they actually offered me the job.*
>
> *It's the only job I've ever done, really. I left college, got married and had a baby. I get job satisfaction. It's pleasant surroundings, pleasant people, the hours suit me, I'm reasonably well paid and it's ten minutes from home.* ❳
>
> Rosemary is 45 with three grown up sons. She works part-time as a dental receptionist and lives in Manchester.

A recent report on working mothers confirms the suggestion that men as well as women are unhappy with the balance of their working and private lives. One in three men and women working more than thirty hours a week would like to work less, and only 4 per cent of women working between ten and twenty-nine hours a week would like to work more.[10]

Confederation of Shipbuilding and Engineering Unions stated that its 1989 campaign to cut the working week from thirty-nine hours to thirty-five was undertaken partly because a growing proportion of men wanted to spend more time at home with their children. The result was a series of negotiated agreements which gave over half a million workers every Friday afternoon off.

One of the most important opportunities that women felt they lacked was flexibility in their working life. The differences between women who had a career and women who did a variety of different jobs to make up their hours was marked: for example, only 10 per cent of profession-als, employers and managers worked part-time.[11] But the report noted that virtually every woman who was offered flexible hours accepted them, and most of those offered the opportunity to work from home did so.

Inflexibility based on outdated male working patterns simply does not suit women. It is assumed that women will complete their careers at sixty – five years earlier than men – even though many women who have spent time caring for children at home are ready to go back into the job market at exactly the age that some employers consider lack of commitment sets in. As Hilary Land, an academic who established her career before becoming a mother, wrote, 'Women who have become more in-terested in their paid work after their children have become less dependent on them, increasingly find that they have just got started when the pressure is on them to leave and make way for a [younger] man.'[12]

Patricia Hewitt outlines the dilemma in her book on flexible working, *About Time*. 'The division of responsibil-ities between men and women at home directly affects the division of opportunities between men and women in employment. Because paid work has first claim on men's time, it restricts the time left for their families: because the family has first claim on women's time, it restricts the time for paid work.'[13]

Twenty-first-century-woman is trying to work within a structure that prevents both men and women balancing work and family. The strategies which women therefore have to adopt to survive within a hostile structure often mean trading money, status and job security for more flexibility and control.

The bias against part-time workers and against women – and the occasional man – who have taken career breaks will have to be challenged if our working culture is to move forward successfully into the twenty-first century. The skills and talents and energies of both men and women are essential, regardless of the number of hours worked, if we are to create the economy Britain needs: an economy which can produce the high-quality goods and services that people want. That is the only way for the British people to enjoy good and rising living standards, to improve our quality of life as a nation, to increase our leisure time and to finance excellent public services.

        ‘ I thought I'd do my bit, have the children and then go back to work. I'd like to go back to being an estate agent, but they are losing people rather than recruiting. At the moment I just help out in my friend's pub and I do a bit of hairdressing, too. I don't mind the pub, but it's not what I want to do. It doesn't use my brain in any way. ’

        Melanie, 35, lives with her husband and two children in Surrey. She used to be an estate agent and now works in a pub.

Companies consider human resources – people and their skills – the most important factor in their future profitability, according to Sylvia Hewlett who carried out a survey of chief executives of top multinational companies for the *Harvard Business Review*. If workers are to be convinced of this we will have to see a new approach from employers, including working patterns that do not penalise mothers, part-timers and older workers. Only then will everyone have the opportunity of working to their full potential – only then will the skills of all workers be valued and our human resources no longer squandered.

Women's Work Counts

Despite the fact that women currently do paid work for fewer hours than men – both the family and the economy rely on women's employment – it is essential to both. In households where only the father has a job, one in six has a gross income of less than £250 per week. When the mother has a part-time job as well, only one in twelve families lives below that limit. Not surprisingly, when both parents are unemployed or the household is headed by a lone parent, almost all families have a weekly income below £250.[14] The number of families classified as poor would treble if mothers did not work. Higher up the income scale, women's earnings are just as essential. In the average family where both partners are earning, the woman contributes at least 25 per cent of the total household income where there are dependent children.

All sectors of industry and service now rely on women's work as well as men's. Even in the male-dominated world of construction, 17 per cent of workers are women; in the metal goods and vehicles industries, 21 per cent are women; and in transport and communications 23 per cent. Four in ten of all manufacturing workers are woman, as are half the people working in banking, insurance, finance, hotels, catering and shops. In other service industries, including schools, hospitals and the public services, two out of every three employees are women.[15]

Part of the reason for this developing picture is the change in all industrial economies. In place of mass production factories, employing thousands of workers to roll

out thousands of identical products, information technology is making it possible to change production lines
and products almost instantaneously. Hard and heavy
work, which was traditionally done by men, is giving way
to technology-based jobs which need skilled workers of
either sex. The shift from mass production to customised
goods, from low-tech to high-tech, from manufacturing to
services – where most women's jobs have traditionally
been found – has been called the post-industrial revolution: two out of three salespeople and personal service
workers are women, as are three out of four secretaries
and clerks.[16]

Even though women's work already accounts for over
40 per cent of Britain's gross national product, and even
though there is legislation covering the principle of equal
pay for work of equal value, women rarely earn the same
as their husbands. The gap is narrowing, but only slowly.
Women's earnings in 1992 were 71.1 per cent of men's
earnings, as compared with 63.3 per cent in 1979.[17] The
gender gap was greater between part-timers. Work in traditionally female-dominated areas, such as childminding
and hospital work, is particularly poorly paid. Most
forms of home-working are also badly paid.

The Council of Europe has set a 'decency threshold' –
the minimum which it believes people should be paid – of
£5.15 per hour. Two-thirds of the workers currently earning less than this sum are women, and the number has increased by more than half a million since 1978.[18]

The losses to women as a result of unequal opportunities, low pay and part-time work are very great. The Low
Pay Unit estimates that British women are being under-
paid by £21 billion as a result of gender bias in employment. And it is mothers who are being most unfairly
treated; Heather Joshi has estimated that the average
earnings of a woman with two children are likely to be
about 30 per cent lower than those of women without
children.[19]

It cannot be stressed too often that it is the presence of
children which makes the difference between women's

work lives and men's. Young men and women with comparable qualifications but who are not parents earn much the same as each other. When men become fathers their earnings are unaffected or increase; when women become mothers their earnings drop. Unequal earnings are the result of unequal responsibilities for the family. When women no longer shoulder the responsibility for children largely unaided, they will be able to apply for jobs that best suit them and their qualifications rather than having to suspend their careers because of motherhood.

Out of Work, Out of Sight

The century gap at work is also demonstrated by the Social Security and National Insurance systems; they too are based on outdated notions of the workforce. The National Insurance payments system was set up in the 1940s to cover people who would be in full-time employment throughout their working lives – that is, men and single women. The Fowler Review in 1985 redesigned Social Security, but did not use the opportunity to reflect the changes in women's working lives since the Second World War. As a result the system does not meet the developing needs of our late twentieth century workforce.

Today's Social Security system is made up of a combination of contributory and means-tested benefits. Claimants who work shorter hours often fall outside the contributory part of the system: according to a 1989 study, between a quarter and a third of part-time employees do not earn enough to be eligible to make NI contributions.[20] The threshold for NI payments, which is lower than that for income tax, means that people who earn a low wage but still fall just above the threshold – common among part-time workers – can find themselves worse off than colleagues on a lower basic wage. This poverty trap creates an incentive for employees and employers to keep declared earnings below the threshold.

People who are not eligible for NI lose out on future

employment, sickness, invalidity and maternity benefit.
A shortfall in contributions can also jeopardise their pen-
sions. NI payments are counted towards SERPS, the state
earnings-related pension scheme. SERPS is currently
based on an individual's best twenty years' earnings, so
that women who spend several years at home or working
considerably reduced hours will not lose out on contributions. However, changes are on the way which will adver-
sely affect such women. For anyone retiring after 1999,
SERPS will be calculated on contributions paid during all
the years spent at work. Anyone who spends between one
and twenty years caring for a child or elderly dependent
and who receives child benefit or invalid allowance can
claim 'home responsibilities protection', which safe-
guards their SERPS contributions. But there are two
problems: first, the protection is only available for whole
years (ignoring the realities of flexible labour); second,
payment of care allowance is subject to restrictions.

Despite the revolution in flexibility of employment, the
unemployment benefit system is still primarily structured
for people who are available for full-time work: recent
changes have only really succeeded in making an unsatisfactory system even more complicated: the regulations do not specify minimum weekly hours, but the clai-
mant is refused benefit it she or he restricts the hours or
days they are prepared to work, or turns down any
'reasonable' job that offers at least twenty-four hours'
work a week. Under this system, someone who wants to
work fewer than twenty-four hours can be forced to work
more, or else cannot register as unemployed; and con-
versely someone who wants to work more than thirty
hours can be forced to work less. The emphasis on weekly
availability ignores the practicalities of annual hours or
term-time contracts. It can be difficult for people on such
contracts, who are usually women, to prove that they are
unemployed in a particular week.

Macho Work Culture

> ❛ When I was pregnant I realised that I wasn't what they called 'star-rated' any more. You had to be totally committed, and they preferred young, single people really. I mean, if you were married that was fine as long as work was No. 1 and you were there from very early until very late, and could be called upon at weekends and all that sort of stuff. For instance, I was phoned from the nursery because Sam had fallen off his bike and the handlebar had gone into his head. He had been taken to hospital, and although they said all the right things I felt I had to go down there. But I also knew that my company didn't want me to go rushing off because I had about six meetings that were all vital. Luckily my husband was able to rush off and do it. ❜
>
> Caroline, 35, is an editor in a publishing company. Married with two children she lives in Oxford.

In many workplaces people are rewarded for the hours they put in rather than what they actually achieve. It is not a question of the number of hours a man or woman is contracted to work, but more that employers often expect their workforce to put in 'extra' hours. In many companies it is the number of hours spent in the office which are taken as a sign of commitment to the job, rather than the quality of the work done. Being at your desk from eight in the morning to eight at night is seen as more important than what you actually achieved that day. This is called 'presentism'. But this macho work culture, with its insistence on long hours for white-collar and manual workers alike, is not conducive to good decision-making, efficiency or even public safety.

Family responsibilities, usually shouldered by women, are often used to justify the assertion that men are more reliable employees. The view is that demanding jobs require enormous flexibility, a willingness to work all hours and availability at short notice. This is seen as applying to middle- and line-management jobs as well as to career jobs.

But, in fact, while there are a few 'response' jobs in-
trinsically of this nature, most of those that become so
are the result of under-staffing, or of bad or crisis
management. Both men and women prove themselves
'indispensable' at work by showing that they are under
huge pressure and have to put in long hours in order to
get the job done. They complain about projects given to
them at short notice, but at the same time do not set out
to challenge the company's structures and are unwilling
or unable to delegate. Most apparently crisis-dominated
jobs could be managed perfectly well within normal
working hours if they were handled in a different way.
Companies which are looking to the future will restruc-
ture so as to get the best out of their employees.

It is women who are least likely to survive the macho
work atmosphere. In management, especially, women find
they have to work extremely long hours, and the more
senior the position the less likely she is to be allowed
options such as job-sharing or shorter hours – or feel able
to take them up without damaging her career. Only 3 per
cent of the women managers interviewed for an Institute of
Management survey in 1992 worked fewer than thirty hours
a week; only 1 per cent had flexible working hours. Nearly
six in ten had never taken a career break.[21]

The same survey confirms that women managers are
more likely to be single than male managers, and much
less likely to have children. In fact, almost two-thirds of
women managers do not have children or other caring responsibilities, whereas almost two-thirds of male
managers do. Nine out of ten male managers are married.
Furthermore, women managers are more than twice as
likely to be divorced or separated than their male
counterparts. The pattern is clear; a man can be a top
manager and have children. A woman cannot unless she
has the good fortune to be married to a man who shares
responsibility at home. As Barbara Brown, Personnel
Manager of the engineering firm Brown & Root, told
Scarlett MccGwire: 'The key to being a successful working mother is choosing the right father.'[22]

The Trade Union Movement

Both management and unions still reflect outdated assumptions about work patterns. Until recently the trade unions, too, were discriminating against women by concluding collective agreements which laid down that in the event of redundancy it would be part-time workers out first and then 'last in, first out'. It was not until this form of agreement was ruled as indirect discrimination, because most of the part-timers were women, in the Clarke versus Ely Kinock case in Birmingham, that such agreements were ended.

A growing proportion of the membership of trade unions is female, reflecting the increasing involvement of women in the workforce, but the leading positions and committees in the movement are dominated by men. Though equality is now on the agenda for discussion, and though many unions have positive action programmes, for the most part they have been slow to translate resolution into practice. The Trades Union Congress, which is a confederation of affiliated unions, has a general council consisting of thirty-five men and fifteen women. At a time when there are nearly equal numbers of men and women in the labour force, it is anachronistic for men to outnumber women on the trades unions' governing body by two to one. But, as in many private and public organisations within Britain, this only reflects the lack of representation of women within unions in general. In the seventy-three affiliated unions there are only two female General Secretaries, despite the fact that there are now several unions in which women members form the majority: the Banking, Finance and Insurance Union has 91,619 women members as against 70,810 men; the Society of Radiographers has 9,611 women and only 3,204 men; the Union of Shop Distributive and Allied Trades and Technicians has 202,289 women members, but only 139,060 men. Despite their preponderance of women members, the General Secretaries of all these unions are men.

Trade unions have an important role to play in protecting workers' rights. They need to attract more women into membership and active involvement, and to participate in shaping changes in response to the growing participation of women in the workforce. If meetings were held in dinner hours rather than after work, and if attempts were made to involve those who could not get to meetings at all, then more women with responsibilities for children would be able to take part; if the needs of part-time workers were taken seriously, then more women would feel that a union had something to offer them too. In 1988–9 the National Union of Journalists, for example, had the first job-share Presidents, Scarlet MccGwire and Barbara Gunnell. The trade union movement has in some instances led attempts to change patterns of employment. Campaigns for equal pay, shorter hours, increased maternity provision and workplace creches have all been either led or supported by the trade union movement. If the unions take steps to try to close the century gap at work, by campaigning on issues of importance to women as well as men – such as increased maternity and paternity leave – then change will come about more quickly, unions will find a new relevance and their members will benefit.

The First Steps

6 I work full-time as a secretary/PA for a small investment company, plus I've got an extra job stringing necklaces. My ex-husband was a jeweller, and his father taught me how to do it and it's extra money. I work most evenings, although sometimes I find it better in the early morning because if I have been on the computer all day at work I really can't see well. 9

Laura, 42, is divorced and lives in Fife with her daughter. She is a full-time secretary and works evenings too.

One of the first steps in overcoming the century gap at work must be to try to change the way in which we think and talk about work. We need to acknowledge that people spend their working lives in a variety of ways: some have careers, some have several part-time jobs, others work from home. We should recognise that there are many different shapes of working lives depending on age, skills and other commitments.

The way we talk about the shape of people's working lives betrays the fact that our thinking is stuck in a time warp. The terms 'part-time' and 'full-time' perpetuate a structure that is now irrelevant. 'Full-time' does not recognise that workers have other aspects to their lives; that we all spend a portion of our time doing something other than paid work. 'Part-time' suggests a less than whole contribution, although there is no evidence that employees who work fewer hours are half-hearted about their jobs. Indeed, one study commissioned by the Post Office, Shell and other large employers found that employers considered staff who job-shared or worked part-time or flexible hours to be more efficient, enthusiastic and committed than their full-time equivalents. And the former Institution of Personnel Management (now the Institute of Management) has found that absenteeism and turnover rates are not noticeably affected by the number of hours worked.

The average operating hours in industry are fifty-eight a week; in theory, anyone who works less than this is part-time. But most of the sources quoted define part-time work as fewer than thirty hours a week. And some 'full-time' workers – such as teachers – officially work *fewer* than thirty hours a week. These terms are no longer accurate and create divisions between groups of working women who otherwise have much in common. In fact, the House of Commons Select Committee on Employment has agreed that the full-time/part-time divide is redundant; instead, the Committee considers our aim should be to offer as many jobs as possible with a range of working hours.

We are more likely to create an accurate picture of the subtle variations in today's labour market if we talk in terms of the number of hours worked a week, or the shape of someone's working life. We must recognise millions of people's demand for differently shaped working weeks at various stages of their lives. Someone who wants to work forty hours a week but can only get a job for twenty is indeed half-unemployed. But someone who wants to work twenty hours a week and gets a job offering just that is fully employed and should be recognised as such.

> *When the children were young I used to go early in the morning to a factory canteen. I was lucky I could take the kids in the pram. I'd butter rolls ready for the workers at break time. Then I got involved with the playgroup which my son was at. I'm qualified as a hairdresser so hairdressing I done on and off from home. Homework I have done odd bits and pieces of that. Cleaning jobs.*
>
> Margaret, 42, has 3 sons and works full-time. She lives in Glasgow.

A reform of working hours would also safeguard employees and the public against the health and safety risks of excessively long hours. There are currently very few legal limits in Britain on the number and combinations of hours that employees are allowed to work or can be required to work by their employers. Denmark and Britain, alone in the European Community, have traditionally regarded working time as a matter for collective bargaining rather than regulation by law. And in opting out of the Social Chapter of the Maastricht Treaty, the Government has made it clear that it does not consider that it has a role in protecting its country's workforce.

Furthermore, the Conservatives have repealed virtually all the protective legislation which covered the working hours of women and children. At present the laws available to women fighting such inequalities are limited to the Sex Discrimination Act, which lays down that a woman must not be treated less favourably than a man; the Equal Pay Act, under which she cannot be paid less for doing the same work or work of equal value; and the EC Equal Treatment Directive, which stipulates that men and women must be treated equally.

Attempts have been made, so far without success, to use those general pieces of legislation to tackle inflexible working practices on the grounds that they indirectly discriminate against women. The Equal Opportunities Commission, for example, has taken a case to the European Court to challenge qualifying periods for employment protection on this basis. In many other cases, the requirement to return to full-time work after maternity leave has been challenged under the Sex Discrimination Act. And a recent Equal Opportunities Report comments that the number of cases – many of them successful – brought under the Sex Discrimination Act against unfair discrimination because of pregnancy has more than doubled in the past few years.[23]

Although, as Linda Dickens argues in *Whose Flexibility?*,[24] such cases have shown that these principles are open to challenge, the disadvantage of using the existing legal routes to create a flexible working climate is that individual women have to prove discrimination and claim compensation for it. They do not start from a position of having right as workers. The European Community's Draft Directive on Part-Time Working, with its principle of equal treatment of all employees regardless of hours worked, does this – but only up to a point.

In its latest form, the Directive is restricted to national and occupational Social Security schemes, holidays, dismissal and seniority allowance. The clauses covering wages, access to promotion and job content have disappeared from the draft since 1983. As Patricia Hewitt says: 'If ... the directive is implemented in its present form, British part-time employees will be left in a thoroughly unsatisfactory position with their terms and conditions decided by a patchwork of employers' discretion, collective bargaining and the operation of the Sex Discrimination and the Equal Pay Acts.'[25]

Despite the fact that in December 1991 the British Government opted out of the Social Chapter of the Maastricht Treaty, European developments are about to impose new conditions on working hours in Britain which will ensure that we start to catch up with the rest of Europe. A compromise proposal for a new European Working Time Directive was agreed by EC ministers in June 1992. Because the Directive is based on article 118a of the Treaty of Rome, which permits qualified majority voting on health and safety issues, it cannot be vetoed by Britain's Conservative Government.

When it comes into effect, the Working Time Directive will include a maximum 48 hour week including overtime, and four weeks' paid holiday a year – pro rata for the number of hours worked. By 1995 the Government will have to put into place the legislation to implement this Directive.

But we in Britain should see this as a positive way forward, and take the opportunity in our Working Time Act to create a new framework for fair flexibility at work. We should also consider introducing pro rata wage rates, conditions of employment and protection rights for all workers, regardless of the hours they work. There will obviously be some increase in wage costs to employers at first, but these should be more than offset by easier recruitment, further reductions in absenteeism and turnover, and the retention of qualified women staff.

Wastage, in both financial and human resources, can be greatly reduced, as a recent report into wastage from NHS nursing shows.[26] Commissioned by the Royal College of Nursing, it highlights the advantages to the economy and to the quality of a service when workers are offered flexible hours, career breaks and the right to return at the same level after maternity leave. Only 17 per cent of nurses return to full-time work after the birth of their first child, compared with 50 per cent of Midland

Bank employees, who are offered a range of flexible working patterns and help with childcare.[27] Since the gross cost of training a nurse over three years is put at £40,000, and the cost of replacing her is estimated at £3,000, this represents a considerable waste of resources.[28]

Nevertheless, as Patricia Hewitt points out, some conditions of the Working Time Directive will need careful handling. Because the forty-eight hour week is an average, which includes a thirteen-hour limit on the average working day and a break of thirty-five consecutive working hours, it leaves the way open for extreme interpretations. For example, under the terms of the Directive an employer could still ask someone to work a seventy-eight-hour working week followed by an eighteen-hour week, or to work a seventy-eight-hour week for seven months of the year.

The equal treatment principle which should be included in a Working Time Act would require employers to open occupational pension schemes to part-time workers or to pay contributions to personal schemes on a pro rata basis. There should also be a way of implementing the EC's proposal that anyone employed for eight hours a week or more should be protected by Social Security and National Insurance.

This sort of initiative will require a shift in priorities. A system of contribution credits similar to those given to unemployed people could be considered. If appropriately organised, this sort of system might also free from the poverty trap employees whose earnings are near the current NI threshold, and offer some protection for their pension. The concept of extending similar protection to people who have taken career breaks could be examined as part of current SERPS policy.

We should overhaul the entire benefits system; it should be aimed at giving equal priority to those who can only find a job for fewer hours than they wish to work and to those unemployed people who only wish to work for part of the week. The needs of those who have caring responsibilities and therefore reduce their hours could also be addressed – particularly married women.

The system for collecting statistics about employment patterns should be changed to allow a clearer picture of the nation's economic activity as we approach the year 2000. In 1985 the United Nations Conference which ended the International Decade for Women called for the inclusion of unpaid work in national accounts, and recently a European Parliament report has recognised that women's unpaid work in the home should be acknowledged as economic activity. It has therefore called for the introduction of childrearing allowances, insurance against the risks of caring for relatives at home, and the accreditation of periods spent raising a family when calculating pension rights.

Sweden, Finland and France all offer parents a right to reduce their working hours while their children are young. In France mothers have a right to return from maternity leave to their previous job or its equivalent, at reduced working hours if they so wish, with pro rata terms and conditions; this is a model which Britain should consider. Parallel arrangements, perhaps offering extended maternity leave, could be considered in the case of small companies for whom the French system would be unreasonably disruptive to business.

Recognising the Value of Older Workers

Career age need not be tied to biological age, and so there should be a flexible decade of retirement. Everyone should be protected against discrimination because of age. One of the first successful challenges to indirect sex discrimination under the 1975 Act forced the Civil Service to raise its limit of thirty-five years for new entrants: it is now a major employer of older women in senior positions.

In Germany, an Older Workers' Part-Time Act in force since 1989 allows anyone to move from full-time to part-time work between fifty-eight and the retirement age of sixty-five. Employers can claim a government subsidy if they recruit unemployed people to make up the older part-timer's hours. In France, a system of half-time employment for older workers is used to create extra jobs. Full-time employees between fifty-five and sixty can move to half-time working and are paid 80 per cent of their full-time salary – half from the employer and the remaining 30 per cent from the Government. The employer has to fill the other half of the post. Such a wide-ranging rethink challenges employers to reject the assumption that most jobs can only be done full-time and makes them consider new opportunities to raise productivity and become more competitive.

The Value of Shorter Working Hours

One possibility, which Hewitt suggests, is that companies should conduct 'working time audits' to check on their progress as they adopt non-standard working time arrangements. Each company should also have a policy which outlines how they plan to help their employees to combine work and family responsibilities. Such a policy might include assessing each job within the organisation to see if it is suitable for shorter working hours, and integrating shorter hours into the career path, with opportunities for promotion.[29]

The flexibility of shorter working hours could also make a contribution to reducing unemployment. A report prepared for the European Commission[30] looks at strategies for economic recovery and reducing unemployment. The researchers set up models which provide options for different approaches to reducing the economic inequalities between different European countries. In order to create more jobs, they have specifically included in those models proposals to reduce by 2.5 per cent annual hours averaged over all employed persons by the year 2000. In this way, increases in productivity would be translated into shorter working hours and more jobs, rather than automatically into pay increases.

Computerisation of personnel and pay records means that flexibility should not be an administrative problem. Nor would shorter working hours be confined to women with young children. Paternity leave would be encouraged, and unpaid career breaks for retraining or family business would be available, with refresher training and suitable hours available on return. Retirement would be flexible, and it would be assumed that employees would reallocate some of their time and money over their working lifetime. The introduction of 'time banks' would help, allowing employees to save a week's salary or more a year during high-earning periods and to use the savings to buy time off later, for family or other purposes.

Towards 2000

Some employers are already beginning to create the twenty-first-century workplace. The Opportunity 2000 initiative, launched by Business in the Community in October 1981, published a summary of equality goals and strategies for sixty-one leading companies. The participants varied considerably in the investment they had already made in addressing family and work issues, and in how specific they were prepared to be about their goals. The *Financial Times* and the *Equal Opportunities Review* checked on their progress six months into the programme and found that those who were specific about their work and family policies highlighted flexible working time arrangements. The Midland and National Westminster Banks and Safeway were moving towards making flexible working available in management jobs. The BBC spoke of targeting such policies at men as well as women.

Lady Howe, who chairs Opportunity 2000, has stressed the importance of the participating companies 'treating women and equal opportunities as a mainstream business issue backed by strong business arguments', and of their backing a stated willingness to change with commitment from chief executive level and with the investment of time, money and resources. In January 1993 the Employment Secretary, Gillian Shephard, launched New Horizons for Women, which drew attention to public appointments as well as paid work as a way of acquiring new employment skills. It aims to develop the equal employment work of Opportunity 2000. Both organisations concentrate, to a certain degree, on high-profile positions. For example, they list that in 1991 there were only three women chief executives, in 1,370 listed companies, whereas by the beginning of 1993 there were five: Ruth Henderson, chief executive of the Alexon clothing group; Anita Roddick, managing director of the Body Shop; Barbara-Anne Maxwell, managing director of the Tamaris nursing homes group; Bridget Towle, joint managing director of the Towle knitwear group; and Michelle Kavanagh, joint managing director of the Irish property company, Power Group.

Although the figures for the number of women occupying senior posts in industry and trades unions are still small, it is important to acknowledge the attempts to close the century gap that are being made. Work and family policies are seen to be firmly in place in the examples of good practice collected by Scarlett MccGwire in *Best Companies for Women*.[31]

In general, the Civil Service, local authorities and the finance and retail sectors lead the way for flexible working. Shorter working hours and job-sharing have been encouraged and expanded in the Civil Service since the early 1980s. In 1991 the proportion of women civil servants working part-time trebled compared with the previous year. Women and part-time employees tend to be concentrated in lower grades, though shorter working hours and job sharing are available at all levels of the Civil Service: there is at least one woman under-secretary working reduced hours. But only 1 per cent of male civil servants work part-time.

In 1983 the Inland Revenue Staff Federation negotiated the opportunity for staff to volunteer for reduced hours. Priority is given to women and men who want to look after children or ill or elderly relatives, or to cope with a domestic crisis, or to wind down their working hours in preparation for retirement. Employees get pro rata pay, holidays and sick leave and retain their pension scheme membership. They can volunteer for fewer hours for specific periods, with the right to return to their previous number of hours. The Inland Revenue found that the scheme helped it to cope with seasonal variations in its workload, and employees were able to move between longer and shorter hours to fit their circumstances. By July 1989, the Revenue was recruiting permanent part-time officers and now all its technical training – the path to promotion – is offered part-time as well as full-time.

Term-time employment has been introduced successfully by, among other companies, Boots the Chemist, which calls it the Flexible Working Parents' Contract. A variation on this is the Alliance and Leicester Building Society's 'V-time' (Voluntary Reduced Time) scheme, which allows full-time employees with children aged between five and fourteen to take time off in school holidays. Overall, a quarter of the women who work only during term-time are employed in education.

There are also some changes in traditionally male-dominated, high-tech businesses. ICI encourages both men and women to take career breaks of up to five years to look after children or elderly relatives, and is prepared to negotiate home-working for new mothers. ICL has a home-working career structure for computer and software developers, who have the same pay and promotion prospects as colleagues who work in the office; while BP offers career breaks and project work at home.

Because technical expertise is scarce, these companies want to attract and retain it. Until now, employers assured of an endless supply of school-leavers have been able to take a short-term view of their staffing requirements. Now, in order to recruit more women and keep them, they need recruitment strategies which offer a choice of working hours and the freedom to vary them over time.

Despite the recession, some women with highly marketable skills are already shopping around to see which employers value their skills most and reflect this by offering the right conditions. Employment consumer guides and league tables aimed at women workers frequently appear in the media. MccGwire's interviewees point to the upward thrust of a new generation of women workers who will not wait for the chief executive to agree an equal opportunities policy. Carol Eastwood, a chief analyst at ICI and a mother, describes her younger female colleagues as 'more demanding and more assured . . . [they expect] nothing short of equality. They are a powerful force for change.'[32]

Employees' enthusiasm about the flexible working practices that have been introduced show that women – and a growing number of men – expect and appreciate an increasing degree of control over when they work. They are seeking ways to vary the hours they work at different times in their lives, especially when children are young, when they want to care for elderly dependants or as they approach retirement.

Companies looking for managers are likely to face an acute shortage of high-calibre recruits.[33] Companies who do not want to lose their share of the best recruits will have to provide the conditions that attract the right women into the right jobs. Failure to keep them there will mean higher costs in turnover, interviewing and readvertising positions. All these costs rise with the seniority of the post. As a Sainsbury spokesperson told *The Independent*: 'A policy of equal opportunities is not entirely altruistic, it is to do with resourcing the business.'

The Institute of Managers stresses the importance of avoiding 'presentism' in enabling women to become senior managers. It calls for 'a redesign of the management career so that results are measured by targets achieved rather than compliance with company culture', and recommends that organisations should discourage out-of-hours meetings and ensure that the decision-making process is accessible to employees who do not want to work after working hours. These changes will happen more quickly if people at the top demonstrate that they have lives to lead outside work.

A further advantage of increased numbers of senior female managers, and one which benefits all women workers, is the reduction of sexual harassment. The Equal Opportunities Commission has shown that incidence is worst in companies where there are few, if any, women in senior management. Some men do take advantage of the power to promote, and pressurise women. Sometimes it is no more than the odd comment; on other occasions it can be as blunt as job opportunities being offered in return for services rendered. In many cases, however, it is the work culture that is to blame. Some men feel that behaviour that was once acceptable – such as flattery about clothes or appearance – has suddenly become classed as harassment. Others, particularly older men, feel uncomfortable when relating to female colleagues of comparable or senior status. As men and women work together on equal terms, sexual harassment will start to be less prevalent.

The Century Gap Closed

The task for Government, management and workers now is to create the opportunities for men and women to look after their families and contribute to the economy. A situation where all men and women can use their skills to the best of their abilities will lead to a more productive and competitive country in an increasingly competitive world. When the century gap closes, we will all be able to afford a better quality of life for ourselves and our children.

Notes

1. Martin, J. and Roberts, C., 'Women and Employment', 1980
2. *Employment Gazette*, March 1990

3. 'Labour Force Outlook to 2001', *Employment Gazette*, April 1990
4. 'Labour Force Outlook to 2001', op. cit.
5. 'Review of the Economy and Employment 1989', Institute for Employment Research
6. Equal Opportunities Commission, 'Women and Men in Britain', 1991
7. Martin, J. and Roberts, C., op. cit.
8. Martin, J. and Roberts, C., op. cit.
9. Handy, C., *The Age of Unreason* (Century Hutchinson, London, 1989)
10. 'Working Mothers: Free to Choose', BSA Report 199*
11. 'Working Mothers: Free to Choose', op. cit.
12. Land, H. in *Being a Mother*, op. cit.
13. Hewitt, P., *About Time*, op. cit.
14. Family Expenditure Survey, 'Women and Men in Britain', op. cit.
15. *Employment Gazette*, November 1992
16. Quantine Database, House of Commons Library
17. New Earnings Survey, 1992
18. 'Women in the Recession': A Labour Party Briefing, September 1992
19. Joshi, H., 'The Cash Opportunity Costs of Childbearing', *Population Studies*, 1990
20. Hakim, C., 'Workforce Restructuring, Social Insurance Coverage and the Black Economy', *Journal of Social Policy*, 1989, Vol. 18
21. Coe, T., 'The Key to the Men's Club: Opening the Doors to Women in Management', an Institute of Management Report in association with British Home Stores, 1992
22. MccGwire, S., *Best Companies for Women*, op. cit.
23. Equal Opportunities Commission Annual Report 1991, 'The Equality Challenge'
24. Dickens, Linda, *Whose Flexibility?*
25. Hewitt, P., op. cit.
26. 'Motivation, Morale and Mobility – A Profile of Qualified Nurses in the 1990s', an Institute of Manpower Studies for the Royal College of Nursing, 1992
27. Davies, C., *The Collapse of the Conventional Careers: The Future of Work and Its Relevance for Post-Registration Education in Nursing, Midwifery and Health Visiting* (ENB, London, 1990)
28. Institute of Manpower Services 'Review of Nurse Turnover Costs', 1991
29. Hewitt, P., op. cit.
20. Stuart Holland European University Institute, Economic and Social Cohesion in the 1990s (Florence, 1992)
31. MccGwire, S., op. cit.
32. MccGwire, S., op. cit.
33. *Employment Gazette*, 1990

Chapter 8

Democracy and the Century Gap

> *Politicians are all a waste of time. They're all too busy making snide remarks about each other's parties. Politics are a waste of time too – well, if we didn't have politics I suppose we'd be in a worse mess than we are in already. It's always men at the head of the Government – well, apart from Maggie Thatcher, and she was a one-off – but I think once women get their teeth into something they will do it.*
>
> Catherine, 40, has one teenage daughter and lives in Carlisle. She works as a secretary.

The century gap has opened up between politics and modern society. Society has changed because the lives of women, and to a lesser extent those of men, have changed. But although the British political system is beginning to adapt to the society it is supposed to serve, our democracy remains unrepresentative. It fails to include half its citizens – women. It's not just a question of giving women the opportunities to become Members of Parliament or local councillors. It's not just about women's issues, such as childcare, being moved higher up the political agenda. It's about democracy being modernised until it fits British society in the 1990s.

Democracy draws its legitimacy from the people it represents. If society changes but that change is not reflected in our political institutions, then democracy itself loses its legitimacy.

During the nineteenth century, men were not only seen

as the moral guardians of women's interests but were their legal protectors as well: a mother and her children were the husband's property in law; women could not own land or buy a house; and they could not vote. Men occupied the public sphere whilst women lived within the private sphere, and the composition of Parliament and local political institutions reflected this division. A small group of propertied men made decisions on behalf of themselves, working-class men and all women.

In 1866, John Stuart Mill presented to Parliament the first petition on the issue of women's suffrage, but it was not until 1918 and the upheavals in society following the First World War that even a limited group of women were given the vote: the Representation of the People Act enfranchised women over thirty, and the Qualification of Women Act in the same year gave women the right to sit in the House of Commons. Countess Markievicz was the first woman Member to be elected, for Sinn Fein, but she did not take her seat. That distinction fell to Lady Astor, a Conservative returned at a by-election who took her seat in the House of Commons in 1919.

But women were still not eligible to vote on the same terms as men. It was not until the 1928 Equal Franchise Act, passed by a Conservative Government led by Stanley Baldwin, that women over twenty-one were given the vote. Another thirty years passed before Harold Macmillan's Government enacted legislation which admitted women to the House of Lords as life peers. Finally, under the Peerage Act of 1963, hereditary peeresses were also admitted to the Lords.

But as the twentieth century progressed women's lives changed dramatically, as did their definition of themselves. Women started to have an identity separate and distinct from that of their husbands. That self-definition takes into account whether or not they are married and whether or not they have children, but by the 1980s this had ceased to be their sole defining characteristic. Their relations with the rest of the world are no longer mediated through their husbands. Nor are many even prepared to concede that their politics are influenced by their husband's. A NOP poll conducted in 1992 just before the General Election revealed that 81 per cent of women stated that their husband's political beliefs did not influence them at all, as against only 67 per cent of men who remained unswayed by the views of their wives.[1]

> 6 *Things would be different if there were more women politicians. Obviously they would do more on issues to do with women – everything like jobs, being treated fairly. They would be more concerned about women. Men politicians, they don't really care, do they? Not as much as women.* 9
>
> Sally is 21 and lives with her sister in London. She is doing a secretarial course.

There is a significant mismatch between the lives of half the citizens of this country and the politicians and institutions which purport to represent them. Our politics now represent a society that no longer exists.

Feminists and other campaigners of previous decades rightly argued, first that it was unfair to deny women the vote, then that it was unfair that there were so few women representatives. This argument is still valid today. But it has been joined by another – that the legitimacy of our democracy is based on its representative nature. If it does not represent our society, then it loses its legitimacy.

The fact that each of Britain's 650 constituencies votes for its own Member of Parliament is an attempt to make the House of Commons representative by ensuring that each geographical area has its own voice. Parliament would be considered profoundly unrepresentative if there were, for example, no MPs from the South-west of England. People there would argue that it was not enough for MPs from other regions to speak up for them – they would want their own voice.

Similarly, if Parliament consisted of 600 women and only 50 men, then men would quite rightly say that they did not want their views reflected only by female MPs and a handful of men. But that is exactly how Parliament looks to women today – unrepresentative. It is no longer any good telling women that men will speak up for their concerns. They want, and expect, their own voice. Mo Mowlam, Labour's Spokesperson on Women, believes that 'unless the lack of faith, trust and confidence in our democratic institutions is addressed, democracy will suffer even more than it is now.'

The Democratic Deficit

❛ I don't think politicians are in touch! They may skim the surface of some things, say education, but half of them haven't an idea what it's like because they're in a better position. I've only got so much money coming in each week, so it's different for me. And the recession – they're not really aware of our feelings. This recession's awful and it's hit everybody, but I don't really think they're aware of how bad it has been. ❜

Lorraine from Sussex is 35 with two sons. She works part-time in a school for children with hearing difficulties.

The politics of both the Left and the Right are going through a period of self-questioning and searching for new directions. There is a sense in the country as a whole that Britain's vicious circle of economic recession and polarisation is symptomatic of a much deeper malaise. Women feel that political institutions, ideas and parties have failed to engage with their changing lives. There have been huge social and economic upheavals – the breakdown of traditional assumptions about the roles of women and men, the changing face of work, industry's new demands for flexibility, the global search for competitive advantage – which government today does not address. As a result, many people swiftly grow bored with listening.

Closing the century gap in politics will refresh and re-
vive a flagging political agenda. And women, as relatively
recent arrivals on the political scene, are less weighed
down with the traditions of the past. They find it easier to
be agents for change, to be a force for realignment of the
politics both of the Left and the right as we enter the next
century.

---

*❡ I'm quite interested in politics. I listen when it's on the telly,
but not intensely. What I'm interested in is mainly about different issues from those which interest men. There's unemployment – that's a major interest because I have an eighteen-year-
old son and he is out of work at the moment. It's a very bleak
outlook for jobs. Every time you hear about different job losses
and things like that it just seems worse for the younger generation. ❡*

Denise, 38, has three children and lives in Hull. She
recently divorced after 19 years of marriage.

The fact that our democracy lacks legitimacy is evi-
denced in the strong sense of disillusion and disinterest
which pervades the public's feelings about politics. The
disillusion is particularly marked among women. It is
paradoxical, but not surprising, to hear women saying
that they care passionately about unemployment, health
care, childcare and education, but that they are not interested in politics. Where women are politically active,
in areas such as getting their local council to provide a
crossing outside a school or obtaining funding for local
play groups, it is often not defined as political activity as
readily as men's trade union or local council activity.

The disconnection between women and our democracy
is exemplified by the woman who only votes because she
feels she ought to, since other women fought so hard to
achieve the vote. Or the woman who goes to vote simply
because her husband does and she goes down to the poll-
ing station with him. They are both voting, though they

may not vote the same way. But in a sense he is voting for a system that he is part of; she is voting in a system that she is not part of.

Democracy for Men Only

That our democracy is male and excludes women can be seen by looking at British power structures – in national and local government, in committees advising decision-makers or in the top ranks of the Civil Service. There has been some progress – but there is still a long way to go. We have had a woman Prime Minister, there are women in the Cabinet, and it is unlikely that an all-male Cabinet would ever be acceptable again. The first woman Speaker of the House of Commons, Betty Boothroyd, was elected in 1992, and the Labour Party elected Margaret Beckett as Deputy Leader in the same year. This would have seemed out of the question even forty years ago. Nevertheless, women in senior positions in politics remain very much the exception. The 1992 General Election saw a record number of women enter the House of Commons as MPs, but, at 60 out of 650 it is still very low: what it means is that some 50 per cent of the population are represented by barely 10 per cent of the politicians.

All the most senior positions in Government are held by men. The Chancellor of the Exchequer, the Home Secretary and the Foreign Secretary are all men – none of these great offices of state has ever been held by a woman. At the time of writing there are twenty men in the Cabinet, but only two women: Gillian Shephard as Secretary of State for Employment and Virginia Bottomley as Secretary of State for Health. Among the twenty-nine ministers outside the Cabinet, only four are women. The Shadow Cabinet is more representative, with five women – Margaret Beckett, Ann Taylor, Ann Clywd, Marjorie Mowlam and me – and there are thirteen women on the Labour Front Bench. Overall in the House of Commons there are twenty women Conservative MPs, thirty-seven Labour women, two Liberal Democrat women and Margaret Ewing for the Scottish Nationalists. This means that roughly 6 per cent of Conservative MPs are women, 13.2 per cent of Labour MPs and 10 per cent of Liberal Democrats. Neither the numbers nor the percentages are impressive.[2]

> ❢ *I don't believe all men make bad decisions. I am not a great feminist, I just think a reasonably equal balance would be lovely.* ❢
>
> Molly is 42 and divorced. She lives in Ayr with her youngest daughter.

Britain has a low proportion of women representatives at the European Parliament in Strasbourg, too. Half of the MEPs from Luxembourg are women, 38 per cent of the Danish MEPs and, 37 per cent of the voting German members – but only 15 per cent of the British contingent.[3] Of the twelve women, seven are from the Labour Party.

Men in government who make public policy appoint men in the Civil Service to implement that policy. In 1992, there were 655 civil servants in grades 1-3 of the Civil Service; of these, only fifty-four, including four of the five part-timers, were women – 8.2 per cent of the total. And male ministers appoint other men to advise them on Departmental Advisory Committees. There are 29,987 men serving on Departmental Advisory Committees and only 9,135 women – 77 per cent men and 23 per cent women.[4]

In theory it should be easier for women to take part in the political process in local councils. Matters such as local schools and tenants' associations have traditionally been regarded as strongholds of women's interest. And the fact that there is not a requirement to travel away from home to Westminster, as there is with MPs, should make the role of local councillor more accessible for women. Yet even in local government the picture is one of male domination.

Of the sixty-two metropolitan authorities, only five currently have women leaders: St Helens, Southwark, Camden, Chelsea and Sandwell; of forty-seven county councils, only four at present have women leaders: Buckinghamshire, Hertfordshire, Humberside and Lancashire.[5] Nine per cent of the non-metropolitan district councils in England are led by women, and 3 per cent of Welsh councils. Four per cent of Scottish district councils are led by women. And the task of implementing council policy within local authorities is headed by a chief executive, of whom at the time of writing 532 are men and only 10 are women.

A 1990 Hansard Society commission report 'Women at the Top' found that 'Britain is almost at the bottom of the league of modern democracies in terms of the proportion of women in the legislature or in the Cabinet. This means that the interests of women are not properly represented in Parliament, in Government, or in Opposition, and that all of us are deprived of women's talents and experiences.'[7] The numbers do matter, because male domination of politics undermines the quality and range of decision-making on women's issues and on matters which concern the effect of public policy on the private sphere of life.

What Are Women's Issues?

I think women politicians have got a lot more sympathy. Like women being told to leave because they are pregnant. I think a lot of men haven't got sympathy with that, because they are not the ones that are going to get pregnant. It must be better to have more women in the long run just because they understand issues like pregnancy and creches for employed people – that sort of thing.

Pam, 38, is divorced. She lives in Wigan with her three teenage children and works in a factory.

If the male domination of politics ensures that women's issues get a low priority, this then begs the question of exactly what a women's issue is. Sometimes women's issues are defined as issues on which all women can be expected to share the same view, but this is too simplistic a definition. Women's issues are those which women are likely to be more concerned about than men – issues which generate more interest and debate among women than men. Abortion is a women's issue, as is the law governing divorce: that does not mean that all women are in favour of abortion or that all men are against a woman's right to abortion. Calling it a women's issue merely acknowledges the fact that it is a subject on which women are more likely than men to hold a view and to hold that view strongly. To argue that women's issues should find a higher place on the political agenda is not, therefore, always to assume any particular outcome.

There are some political issues which are gender-neutral – which both men and women feel strongly about – such as unemployment. But even on these gender-neutral issues, women's perspective of women may be different; for example, a woman's concern about unemployment is more likely to be expressed in personal terms to do with her family, whereas for a man it may be worry about losing his own job. The involvement of women with the care of their children means that many political issues are looked at through the perspective of the family as well as through her own eyes as an individual.

6 *Well, I worry about unemployment. I have been a Tory all my life and I can't believe they are doing this. My middle son, he has just been made redundant. I mean, the building trade has just died. I mean, he will take any work, but he just can't get anything. I am really worried about the state of things at the moment.* 9

Rosemary is 45 with three grown up sons. She works part-time as a dental receptionist and lives in Manchester.

Some issues are women's issues, but are not seen as such. For instance, it is women for the most part who work in shops, and women who do the shopping, and yet the question of Sunday trading is not seen as a women's issue. And it will be an overwhelmingly male Parliament which will decide on whether and which shops should be allowed to open on Sunday, and what the balance should be between legal protection for those who work in shops and the needs of other working women who cannot shop during the week.

It is not merely that women's issues are not given sufficient importance; confining the discussion of some issues to men distorts the debate. Men MPs can confidently debate contraception when it is seen as a Third World issue of development and population control. But they are happier to avoid the debate, as it touches their wives and daughters who have to deal with contraception in their everyday lives.

Part-time work is another issue which a male Parliament of more than full-time MPs simply cannot get right. It is not just a matter of insufficient attention being given to the importance of part-time work and to the need to improve the terms and conditions of part-time workers; difficulties also arise because part-time work is often seen either as marginal by Conservatives or as problematical by Labour MPs. It is not long since Labour Shadow Secretaries of State for Employment were openly hostile to part-time work, which they saw only as an employer's device to undermine the terms and conditions of full-time employees. When Conservative ministers announce the creation of new jobs (usually to divert attention from the unemployment figures) some Labour MPs can be heard to call out: 'But they are only part-time jobs' – meaning that they don't count. There is no reflection in Parliament of the strong commitment which women part-timers bring to their work, the importance of their income to their families, and the fact that for many women part-time work is their *choice* because they want to be able to combine work with the care of their children. Part-time work as a problem appears on the political agenda, and part-time workers having problems through lack of rights sometimes appear on the full-time male agenda. What fails to appear is the understanding that part-time work is not just a problem, but a work pattern for the future.

Government decisions create and shape the labour market. If the decisions are made by men understanding only male patterns of employment, the resulting legal framework discriminates. It is not only in order to make our democracy representative that we need both men and women in politics, not only to ensure that half the population believes it is their democracy as well. We need both men and women to ensure that the decisions made by Government reflect the world as it is.

> Many men don't see women adding something to the greater whole. They only see that women will take something from them. That's the way it operates. They don't value the difference and they don't see the additional dimension women bring to the discussion. On an individual level they might acknowledge it, but within institutions they cannot see women as carrying the same weight as men.[8]

Women Voters

❛I quite often support Labour – I changed from SDP. It depends, really. At the moment, as I say, I'm a bit confused. It's all up and down – you don't know from one week to the next what's happening. If they would only put it into plain English, you would understand. Some of them are better at explaining things than others, but some of them come on the television and you think they come from a different planet.❜

Shona is 39 and divorced with two teenage sons. She works in a home for elderly in Aberdeen.

Opinion polls show that in this country women are the "switch" voters. Though many do have traditional loyalties to one or other of the parties, particularly those whose parents – often fathers – followed party politics closely, women are more likely than men to switch between parties from election to election. The level of cynicism about politics and politicians generally is markedly higher among women than men.

❝ *I voted for the Conservative Party, but I don't think that was through anything of myself. I think it was more Mum and Dad, and I sort of followed them. Is there a party that is doing something about childcare and fights for women and also student grants as well? Those issues do affect me.*❞

Nicola is 20 and a university student. She lives with her parents in Reading.

Clearly the political allegiance of women and their votes are prizes which have yet to be won. The question is whether the presence of women candidates and women MPs could make inroads into the high level of disaffection about politics among women.

The election of Margaret Thatcher in 1979 as the first woman Prime Minister of the United Kingdom and the first woman Prime Minister in western Europe had a significant impact on women in this country. In 1975 she had already broken new ground by becoming the first woman leader of a political party in this country. Yet, when driven from office in November 1990, she left behind her an all-male cabinet. It is hard to know whether her statements berating women for not using their opportunities were born out of a desire to encourage women to press on, or were simply a triumphant assertion that she could do it and if other women couldn't it was their own fault.

> *Even though Margaret Thatcher was one of the sort that had to be twice as good as a man and more like a man than anyone else, in her own way she did show that there could be a woman in that role.*
>
> Caroline, 35, is an editor in a publishing company. Married with 2 children she lives in Oxford.

But the very fact that she was a woman and had become Prime Minister was of enormous significance, particularly for women. She evoked strong responses – people either loved or hated her. But her ascent to the office of Prime Minister was a signal, particularly to women, that there was no ceiling – that once a woman had been Prime Minister it could never again be said that a woman 'can't do it', and that even if their own lives were limited they nevertheless belonged to a gender who were now equal to any man. The assertion that it was acceptable to exclude women because of their gender was driven even further underground.

It is paradoxical that the election of the first woman Prime Minister gave enormous confidence to women about their potential achievements, but at the same time reduced their chance of following in her path by cutting legal maternity rights for working women. She even opposed the Directive from the European Commission which required the law in all EC countries to give women a legal right to claim equal pay for work of equal value; the Directive subsequently did find its way through the Commission and thereafter had to be incorporated in British law.

Women in power will not necessarily make decisions that appeal to all women, of course. Many are uncomfortable with the idea of positive action, while others are worried about the idea of being ghettoised if they try to support women as a group, as distinct from men. In their excellent analysis of women and politics, Anna Coote and Polly Pattullo quote an example of the hostility felt by many men and women towards initiatives designed to promote women:

> Traditional attitudes die hard. Janice Rose, a Women's Aid worker in Sheffield, remembered a discussion at her local Labour Party meeting on whether to set up a women's section. 'This bloke stood up and said, "My wife's not here at the moment, but I know that she fully agrees with me and she's totally against them because they're so cliquey." I said, "What's she doing at home?" he said, "Well, we have got a family you know."[9]

Some women are concerned that positive action to ensure the entry of more women into politics will constitute tokenism and debase women's political involvement in general. However, most women do think that a greater representation of women in politics will make a difference to their lives. President Clinton recognised this in his election manifesto, *Putting People First*, when he pledged to 'hire and appoint more women at all levels of government, so that a Clinton–Gore Administration better reflects this country's population.'[10]

The argument that politics is unrepresentative without the involvement of women is not new. As long ago as 1929 the General Secretary of the Labour Party Women's Organisation urged the Labour Party conference that more women candidates needed to stand for election. The arguments have gained ground and gathered support over the decades. Those prepared to challenge the arguments have found that there are fewer places now where they can express those views openly. Organisational changes have been put in place to underpin those arguments, even though attitudes still lag behind. As Labour MP Jean Corston said:

> It wasn't so long ago that a senior Labour male politician was talking to me about a committee that was going to be established, and he ran through the membership and asked me what I thought. I said it was great, but wasn't there any room for, say, Jo Richardson? He looked at me and said, 'That's a good idea and we could have other minorities as

well, couldn't we?' That certainly wouldn't be said on TV now, but it is still said here because that's the view.[11]

The changes that will narrow the gap between women and politics and will modernise our democracy by reflecting the changes that have taken place in society will be made eventually. The trend is already discernible, and changes are already taking place through competition between political parties for women's votes, through organisational changes to promote women, through the actions of women representatives and as a by-product of closer European integration. The important thing now is to accelerate the pace of those changes.

> *I care who is in power, yes, and I think women should vote. When women say they don't vote – well, I think they should vote. When you think of what women went through to get us the vote, I just don't understand.*
>
> Sheila, 41, has one son and lives in London with her husband, a welder.

The Spur for Change

Change has already taken place as parties become more sophisticated about the process of winning votes at elections. All parties now specifically address themselves to the question of winning the votes of women. Even if they are, in principle, against the separate identification of 'women's issues' and, in theory, feel unconcerned about the under-representation of women, the very process of focusing on winning women's votes seems to go hand-in-hand with organisational changes that increase or strengthen women's representation. Some male politicians may not really want to see more women in Parliament, they may believe that a woman's place is in the home looking after her husband and family, they may not feel that women's opinions are as important as men's. But as politicians they cannot afford not to try to gain the support of women voters.

Talk of 'targeting women's votes' sounds like a hostile process. But, even if the intention is purely cynical and aims to do nothing more than win an election, merely thinking along these lines in itself contributes to the process of change.

The Conservatives pour scorn on the proposal for a Women's Ministry, yet in his 1992 Government John Major gave a Cabinet minister, Gillian Shepherd, special responsibility for women's issues. It is not, it appears, possible to address the question of winning women's votes without conceding ground to the arguments for greater representation for women. So, on of the principal engines for change is the recognition among all parties of the need to win women's votes and to adopt specific strategies to do so.

The process of change takes place within each party. But change in one party affects the others. The fact that the Conservatives were led by a woman was undoubtedly a spur to action in the Labour Party. It was uncomfortable for Labour – a party committed to the principle of equality for women – to have so few women in their leadership team. In another instance, it was change in the Labour Party that precipitated change in the Conservative Party. In November 1989, Neil Kinnock wanted to increase the number of women in the Shadow Cabinet; there was only one at the time, the veteran women's rights campaigner Jo Richardson. The problem was that Labour MPs would not vote in large enough numbers for their female colleagues. So Neil Kinnock drove a rule change through the Parliamentary Labour Party, which required all MPs to include at least three women on their ballot paper for the Shadow Cabinet election; failure to vote for at least three would result in the ballot paper being declared invalid. As a result the number of women in the Shadow Cabinet increased from one to five. At the time of writing it contains five women and twenty-four men.

Once the Labour Party had undertaken this rule change it became impossible for John Major to have no women at all in his Cabinet. His first Cabinet was all-male, and met with adverse comment in the newspapers; it was clear now an all-male Cabinet no longer looked right. It was inevitable at the first reshuffle that women would enter the Cabinet and indeed they did, with Gillian Shephard's appointment as Secretary of State for Trade and Industry and Virginia Bottomley becoming Secretary of State at the Department of Health.

> *❝ I would like to see some support for women who stay at home to have their children, like in other European countries. If this was extra money it would be like a dream, like Switzerland or other European countries who do pay or give their mothers something to stay at home. If they can have it, why not us? ❞*
>
> Stephanie is 34, married with three children. She works part-time in a post office and lives in Kent.

Just as change in one political party triggers change in the others, then closer integration with the rest of Europe will prompt new ways of thinking about things in Britain. As people start to be more aware of the day-to-day lives of their European neighbours, comparisons will increasingly be made: in nursery provision, in maternity and paternity leave, in workers' rights and in the proportion of women actively involved in politics.

Many parties in other European countries have introduced quota systems: the Austrian Social Democratic Party has a minimum of 25 per cent women representatives, Denmark has a minimum of 40 per cent for both women and men, while the Portuguese Socialist Party has introduced a 25 per cent minimum quota. And the fact that other European countries have more women representatives at all levels not only shows that these initiatives can work, but also makes it clear that the current

British pattern of representation is not inevitable. The Labour Party is already including quotas at all levels, the target being 41 per cent women by 1995.

The Treaty of Rome enshrines in law the principle of men and women receiving equal pay for equal work. The Social Chapter of the Maastricht Treaty, agreed by the eleven other member states of the European Community, but not by Britain takes the challenge one step further in stating that 'The community shall support and complement the activities of the Member States in equality between men and women with regard to labour market opportunities and treatment at work.'[16] As British women see their European counterparts enjoying the benefits of such legislation, they will start to question the decisions that excluded them.

One measure that has been canvassed as a way of introducing more women into Parliament is electoral reform. But the significant Plant Report – a Labour Party working party on electoral reform which was published in 1991 – concluded that:

> We are not so far convinced that electoral systems in themselves will make a tremendous difference to the greater representation of women ... Clearly there is evidence from some countries that list systems either as pure lists or in the form of AMS [Additional Member System] have a better record in securing better female representation, but this does depend crucially upon a) the attitude of the party which determines the list; b) the general position of women and other groups in society and the extent to which they have wider opportunities. In our view, while electoral systems may be enabling conditions, the procedural justice of electoral systems has to draw upon a more substantial degree of social justice in society.[17]

Redefining a Good MP

The traditional definition is based upon the assumption that the good MP has made a choice between Parliament and his family, and chosen Parliament. The good

MP – 20th century style – has time for his family, but in
any contest they must be put second to his party and his
constituents. The good twenty-first-century MP will
recognise that decisions in the public sphere affect life in
the private sphere, and that he or she should not be cut
off from the new society which has taken on board
changes in the relationship between work and home, and
between men and women.

The stereotype of a good Conservative MP is someone
whose wife organises social functions in the constituency
on his behalf and is able to bring up his children, so that
he can give his undivided attention to his constituents
and his career. Emma Nicholson MP describes a selection conference at which one of the committee members
confided that she had rejected the first woman on the
shortlist because she had children, and would therefore
not be able to give her undivided attention to the constituency. Yet Emma was subsequently rejected as un-
acceptable because she was *not* married with children. It
was not 'normal' – too many questions would be asked
about her. Neither the unmarried woman nor the married
woman conformed to the picture of a good MP.

The stereotype of a good Labour MP is someone whose
commitment is demonstrated by working seven days a
week. His wife is busy with the children and talking on
the phone to his constituents when he is in Westminster
or out at a meeting. His commitment to socialism is evi-
dent simply on the basis of the number of hours he works.

It goes without saying that everyone wants the best MP
possible. But judging simply by the number of hours
worked does not tell you anything. There have been MPs
who are workaholic, but who fail in every other respect. It
is possible to be an ineffective MP and a workaholic but it
is not possible to be a mother of small children and a workaholic, unless the children are sacrificed.

As in all spheres of work, what matters is the quality of
the MP's efforts, not merely the quantity. Quality of work
is undermined by tiredness through constant work. And
the quality of representation is undermined if MPs are

excluded from the changes that are taking place in the lives of their constituents. John Garrett writes that in 1983 the Top Salaries Review Body 'found the average hours worked per week by an MP were sixty-nine when the House was sitting and forty-two when it was in recess, giving an average of sixty-two for the year'. Such hours reinforce the idea that Parliament is a 'man's job' – where else would you expect to find women working a sixty-nine-hour week? 'Such hours', he continues, 'also act as a deterrent to the recruitment of women members.'[18a]

The difficulties imposed on those who want to combine family responsibilities with Parliament are increased by the question of where the MP should have his home, 'home' being defined as where the wife and children live. At selection conferences, party members are keen to ensure that their prospective MP will have a strong commitment to constituency activity. This concern is born out of a fear – and sometimes past practice – that, once selected and safely elected, the MP will be off to Westminster and forget his constituents and his local party. It is, of course, important that this should not happen. But absolute priority given to MPs having their home in the constituency can amount to indirect discrimination against women.

Prospective candidates from outside the constituency are asked to promise to move their wife – or husband – and children into the constituency. And local candidates are pressed to promise that their family will stay in the constituency and not move to be with him in London. This often results in a man moving his family into the constituency, as a way of expressing his commitment to it, at a time when he is moving to London for a substantial part of his life. This is possible, though not desirable, for some men to do; it is possible for only a few women.

Local parties need bear in mind that in selecting an MP they are selecting not only someone to represent their own area, but someone who will be part of the representation of the whole nation. If hardly any of the local parties select women they are contributing to the weakness of our democracy.

When selecting their candidate, it is important for local parties not to discriminate against women by discounting relevant political experience. Trade union action – mostly the province of men – is seen as political action and appropriate experience for becoming a political representative. Action in tenants' associations – mostly undertaken by women – is not so readily defined as political experience. Both tenants' action and trade union action involve many of the same skills. Yet the male world of the trade unions is seen as political, while the female world of tenants' associations and playgroup committees is not. As Cynthia Cockburn comments in her important book *Women, Trade Unions and Political Parties*, it is harder for women to break into the world of politics, especially trade union politics, than it is for men. 'The role model for unionism is male. Even women activists, it has been found, are more likely than non-activists to have fathers or husbands who have had a tradition of trade union belonging. It was seldom their mothers that passed the trade union tradition on to women.'[20] And since many women have not led conventional working lives, but have spent time bringing up a family, unless their different experiences are valued it will be difficult to break the mould.

Parliament: For Women and Men

The way Parliament works is not compatible with bringing up children. Many MPs are able to delegate their day to day parental responsibilities to their wives. But that is not a step that most women are able – or willing – to take.

There are a number of reforms which, as well as modernising Parliament and making it more efficient, would make Parliament more accessible to women MPs.
- Changing the Parliamentary week to include more days in the constituency and fewer in Westminster

- Changing the times at which Parliament sits, from afternoon and night, to morning and afternoon
- Changing the times of the Parliamentary recess to co-incide with school holidays
- Establishing arrangements for MP's to have maternity and paternity leave.

Changing the Parliamentary week would reflect the recognitgion of the growing importance of an MP's work in the constituency, as well as making it easier to combine being an MP with bringing up a family.

Parliament currently sits four and a half days each week. This could be changed to 3 days in Westminster and 2 days in the constituency.

There is a reluctance among some MPs to press for a change in the balance of work between Westminster and the constituency, because of the justified fear that this will be interpreted as laziness. Any MP who raised this issue could be vilified in the press and arouse suspicion among his or her constituents. So male MPs suffer isolation from their families, which limits their ability to understand and therefore contribute to policy development on issues which affect the home. And some women are not prepared to put themselves in the position where they feel they have to choose between their children and a parliamentary career, so they do not seek selection.

It is questionable whether the House of Commons really needs to sit for as many days of the year as it does at present. More decisions could be taken at a local level. As well as decentralising decision-making, this would reduce Westminster's workload.

The US Senate and the Canadian lower house sit for only half as long as the British House of Commons, and the Parliaments of Germany and Italy are in session for an even shorter time. So why not Britain?

It is long overdue to change the times at which the House of Commons sits.

At present the Chamber of the House of Commons is in session from 2.30pm to approximately 11pm Monday to Thursday. Sometimes it remains in session until the early hours of the morning. The Friday session runs from 9.30am to about 3pm to allow MP's to travel to their constituencies for the week-end.

The sitting times of the House of Commons have changed over time. In the 16th century, The House of Commons sat in the mornings, and afternoons were reserved for the work of committees. During World War II, the House reduced its hours to save fuel, meeting at 11am and sat until 6pm. The present sitting times date from 1945.

It is argued by some who oppose change in the sitimg times that they must remain as they are to allow MP's to do another job during the day and therefore keep in touch with the world outside Westminster. But constituency work is far more likely to keep an MP in touch with the real world than being a barrister or being a Director of a Merchant Bank, which is what some MP's do during the day.

The increasing demands of the constituency mean that if an MP is able to fit in another job as well as his work in the constituency and in Westminster, he probably is not fully performing his role as MP.

And night sittings do deter women who want to be able to work during the day but be at home in the evening with their family.

A report into the Select Committee on the Sittings of the House was published in February 1992, and was the clearest indication so far that male as well as female MPs were unhappy with the restrictions places on their lives outside Parliament because of the structure of their working week. This, the report concludes, 'reveals a desire among Members to have a working live with more predictable and less anti-social hours'[18]

Some industries and services require night working, but there is no justification for night working in Parliament. It only succeeds in lowering the quality of debate, and is merely a relic of tradition that prevents us from taking Parliament forward in a fit state to face the demands of the twenty-first century.

We also need to change the time that the House of Commons takes its summer break. The House rises for the summer recess at the end of July, or beginning of August and returns half way through October. English and Welsh MPs are therefore in Westminster for half their children's school holidays and as school holidays are even earlier in Scotland, the MP's from Scotland go home for the recess after their children have already begun the Autumn Term. There is no reason to persist with recess times which prevent MP's being based in their constituencies during their children's school summer holidays.

Mothers in the Mother of Parliaments

If we want women to be in Parliament, and if we expect to include young women as well as older ones, then we must also expect some of them to have children. It is recognised in the world of work outside Westminster that women who have babies need maternity leave and that arrangements must be made accordingly. Similarly, there should be maternity leave of some kind in Parliament; at present it is left to the woman herself to negotiate with her constituency and the Whips. When an MP is ill arrangements are made, sometimes for far longer than would be necessary for maternity leave. The ill MP is 'paired' with an MP from the other party, while constituency responsibilities are shared with neighbouring MPs or local councillors from the same party. These arrangements work perfectly well on a temporary basis, so there seems no reason why there should not be a system of maternity leave working on similar lines.

Selecting Women Candidates

Organisational changes within the political parties which have been attempted include direct and indirect intervention in the selection process. The Conservatives have

taken special measures to identify, to put on their
national list of candidates and to give special help to,
women whom they feel have the best chance of being
selected. Labour requires all parties to include at least
one woman on every shortlist for selection of a candidate.
In addition, informally through Labour Women's Network, and formally through the party's Organisation
Department, special training and assistance is available
to women seeking to be candidates. Labour Women's
Network, an informal organisation within the party, is
establishing EMILY's list, an idea borrowed from the
women in the US Democratic Party.

EMILY's List

Emily's list was developed in the USA as a means of getting more Democrat women elected to high public office,
EMILY's List does not support all women democrats, but
only those who have declared themselves in favour of the
right to abortion and the Equal Rights Amendment, an
amendment to enshrine in the Constitution.

Women face a particular disadvantage in the US political system, since the route to office can be barred to those
who do not have large funds for election campaigns.
EMILY (an acronym standing for Early Money Is Like
Yeast – meaning that it increases considerably in size)
funds women's campaigns through a network of 23,000
members. Membership doubled in the wake of the Cla-
rence Thomas hearings in 1991 in which Thomas, the
President's candidate for Supreme Court judge, was
accused of sexually harassing a female colleague. In 1986
the group raised 350,000 and helped Barbara Mikulski of
Maryland become the first woman to be elected to the US
Senate. In 1990 it raised $1.5 million and helped to elect
two women governors, Ann Richards of Texas and Barbara Roberts of Oregon, as well as three women Democrats to the House of Representatives; this increased the
number of women in that body to a record 20 out of a

total of 435. The Republican Party had a similar organisation called WISH (Women in the Senate and House).

EMILY's List was launched in Britain in February 1993. It consists of a list of women whom they are committed to help get selected as Labour MPs by offering help towards election expenses to the local party that selects them. This is analagous to being included on Labour's A List, the list of candidates who have already attracted a financial commitment from a trade union. In these cases, the union pays an annual sum to their constituency and pays a substantial contribution to election expenses if they are selected. Traditionally, there have always been substantially more men than women on the A List, giving constituency Labour parties a financial incentive to select a man.

Barbara Follett, who took the initiative to launch EMILY's List in the UK, believes that giving local constituency Labour parties a financial incentive could help get more women selected as candidates. Also, women need help with the basic costs of seeking election. Follett says:

> In politics, as in almost any other walk of life, women have to work twice as hard and be twice as good as men if they want to succeed. Because women earn less than men and have more family responsibilities, money is vitally important. Many able and articulate women cannot even consider applying for a constituency because the transport and child-care costs of attending the thirty to forty selection meetings involved in each section are simply too high.

New Procedures

If it is clear, as it should be, that we cannot have so few women MPs, there has to be a commitment to a change that will work. Simply lessening women's disadvantages have not been enough to overcome the entrenched patterns. So whatever the other advantages or disadvantages of electoral reform, it seems that the electoral system itself is not the factor that determines how many women there are in Parliament. Changes in the way political parties select candidates seem to be more important. One certain way to ensure that more women enter Parliament from all regions of the country is for political parties to decide that, when an MP from that party retires, they will select a women as their next candidate. They will have an all-women shortlist.

This proposal has been canvassed and met substantial hostility within the Labour Party. There are arguments against it which appear more frequently than any others: that it will reduce the quality of candidates by excluding men; and that it is unfair on men, many of whom have been working long and hard to get themselves into a position where they can be selected, only to see their chance disappear just because of their gender. It is often added that you cannot improve democracy by resorting to methods which cut across it.

As to the first argument, there are plenty of women within the Labour Party who could be excellent MPs, too. On the second point, some excellent men would not get selected; an excellent woman would be getting the chance instead. If more women enter Parliament, that is a price worth paying. If evolutionary change means progress that is so slow as to be imperceptible, then more radical measures have to be taken.

As to the objection that it is anti-democratic to interfere with the selection choice of local parties, that argument assumes that what we have at present is a properly functioning democracy. But democracy is clearly not functioning properly since women remain so under-represented. Simply waiting for the process to change of its own volition has already taken too long, and further damage will be done to democracy as the legitimacy of the system weakens further. All-women shortlists would redress the imbalance of having, for so many years, so many all-male shortlists.

What Role for the Role Models?

❛ I've always admired Clare Short when she took on all those men that were so awful to her and she had to withstand that terrible personal campaign. I am always quite admiring of women who take on these roles, because I think a lot of women are not allowed to feel that comfortable in the City world so I was really pleased that Margaret Beckett took on that role. ❜

Maria is 35 with twin daughters. She is a journalist and lives with her husband in Hertfordshire.

Women political representatives are in a very small minority, and there is, of course, some debate about what role they should play, if any, on the issue of representation of women. Two opposing views are urged upon women politicians, with equal fervour: that they should speak up for women and focus on women's issues; or that their duty is to succeed, and the way to succeed is to avoid being marginalised and stereotyped as 'only interested in women's issues' by concentrating on matters which have traditionally been close to the male heartbeat.

The answer is that women politicians need to do both, to speak up on women's issues *and* contribute to the so-called mainstream of political debate. If women politicians do not speak up on the representation of women and on women's issues, inevitably the issue will remain buried. Left to themselves, it is unlikely that men will focus on issues that are important mainly to women. Women politicians, because of their small number, do have a responsibility for the representation of women who otherwise see no reflection of their lives in the political process. At a time when change is happening, but only slowly, women politicians have to be agents for change. But that does not mean that they can allow themselves to be excluded from the mainstream. In order to

change the hearts of politics they need to be part of it –
not, as Margaret Thatcher saw it, to beat men at their
own game, but to change the rules of the game.

Men Learning to Share Power

Men in politics are used to negotiating with and sharing
power with other men, but they are not used to sharing
power with women. Modernising our democracy by recognising the changed role of women will also require
men in politics to change. They will need to become as
accustomed to dealing with a woman who is their equal
or their superior as they are to dealing with other men on
those terms. As Joan Ruddock says: 'Male domination of
politics is subtle. Essentially it is about men inclining to
support, vote for, choose, give credit and authority to
their own sex over women. In most contexts men psycho-
logically don't see women as holding equal status.'

It is difficult to encourage the acceptance of the prospect of power-sharing between men and women at a time
when some men are feeling threatened by the issue of
adequate representation of women. Men will be especially unwilling to share power if they feel that the
women are not up to the job and are only there because of
a desire for positive action in favour of women. This is
not to say that positive action is not important – it is. It is
merely to emphasise that it is counter-productive to
appoint or promote a woman who is incapable of a particular role simply because she is a woman. That is unfair
on her, setting her up to fail, and it sets back the argument for modernising our democracy by allowing men to
point out that a particular woman has failed. Many men
fail. But women's failures are more visible because there
are so few of them. All women in public office are role
models to other, particularly younger, women. It is therefore important to make the right choices so that the
models will be positive.

A Ministry for Women

❝I get mixed up as to whether positive discrimination for women is a good thing or not a good thing. It depends which report you have read recently.❞

Caroline, 35, is an editor in a publishing company. Married with two children she lives in Oxford.

A proposal for a Women's Ministry was included in Labour's election manifestos in 1987 and 1992. Subsequently, the proposals have come under fire from within the Labour Party as well as from the Conservatives.

In trying to transform our institutions following on a transformation that has taken place in society there are no obvious and easy answers, no guaranteed solutions.

When there are women ministers in all Government departments, equal numbers of men and women in the Cabinet and in the higher reaches of the Civil Service, it will not be necessary to have specific measures. But the functions that have been identified for the Women's Ministry are important, monitoring the impact of the policies of each department on women; co-ordinating the work on women by the women ministers in each department; establishing goals and targets and reporting to Cabinet. There have been attempts in a number of other countries to try and ensure that male-dominated political institutions do not discriminate against women. In Canada, every cabinet proposal has a statement on its impact on women and in Germany the Ministry for Women's Affairs has responsibility for equality law and maternity protection.

These functions are probably best served by having a Cabinet member responsible for women, monitoring all departments and reporting to Cabinet. This is what the Conservatives now do, having followed the precedent set by Labour when Jo Richardson MP was given responsibility within the Shadow Cabinet for women's issues. It is what the voters, women and men alike, now expect from the politicians.

The Century Gap Closed

When the century gap is closed, politics in Britain will look and feel completely different. Political representation, at all levels, will be by equal numbers of men and women. When the century gap is bridged, there will be no need for positive action because our male democracy will have been replaced by one that is both male and female. Organisational changes to deal with the lack of representation of women are only necessary as transitional measures. Thereafter, men and women will be judged on merit alone and by the skills and qualities they can bring to their political work.

Debate in Parliament will more accurately reflect debate in the country, as Parliament demonstrates a new ability to discuss issues such as childcare, contraception and flexible working hours with as much confidence and authority as it now debates the economy and foreign affairs.

The closing of the century gap will not only put Parliament in closer touch with the people, it will put the people in closer touch with the issues decided in Parliament. Women debating the economy in Parliament will be listened to by women at home looking after children. They will know it has just as much to do with them as with their husbands.

There should be no question that this represents an advance. It offers the chance of making the political process relevant to the nation as it now exists. Politics will be for all the people. The question is not whether we should, or will, go in this direction. The question is simply how fast we can make the changes necessary.

> *If there were more women MPs I think things would be balanced out. There would be more of an even feel rather than a sort of dominated feel to everything.*
>
> Trudi, 35, lives in Brighton with her three children. She is working as a cleaner while she retrains in computers.

Notes

1. NOP Poll reported in *The Independent*, 18 March 1992
2. House of Commons Library, 1993
3. European Parliamentary Office, London, 1992
4. Public Bodies 1991
5. Association of Metropolitan Authorities and Association of County Councils 1992
6. Municipal Yearbook 1992
7. Hansard Society, 'The Report of the Hansard Society Commission on Women at the Top', 1991
8. Coote, A. and Pattullo, P., *Power and Prejudice: Women and Politics* (Weidenfeld & Nicolson, London, 1990)
9. Clinton, B. and Gore, A., *Putting People First*, op. cit.
10. Causton, J., interview with Harriet Harman, January 1993
11. Ruddock, J., interview with Harriet Harman, January 1993
12. *Financial Times*, 11 November 1990
13. Mahon, A., interview with Harriet Harman, January 1993
14. Abdela, L., *Women with X Appeal: Women Politicians in Britain Today* (Macdonald Optima, London, 1989)
15. Vallance, E., *Women in the House: A Study of Women Members of Parliament* (Athlone Press, London, 1979)
16. Article 2 of the Social Chapter, Protocol to the Maastricht Treaty, 1989
17. Plant, Professor R., 'The Plant Report: A Working Party on Electoral Reform', July 1991
17a. Garrett, John, *Westminster: Does Parliament Work?*
18. Select Committee Report on the Sittings of the House, Vol. I, 18 February 1992
18a. Garrett, J., op. cit.
19. Primarolo, D., interview with Harriet Harman, January 1993
20. Cockburn, C., *Women, Trade Unions and Political Parties*, Fabian Research Series no. 349

Select Bibliography

ABDELA, L., *Women with X Appeal* (Macdonald Optima, London, 1989)

BURCHILL, J., *Ambition* (Bodley Head, London, 1989)

CAMPBELL, B., *Wigan Pier Revisited* (Virago Press, London, 1984)

CHESTER, R., *Divorce in Europe* (NIDI Martinus Nijhoff, Leiden, 1977)

CLIFT, C. and FIELDING, D., *The Balance of Power* (Lowe Howard-Spink, London, 1991)

PAHL, J., *Money and Marriage* (Macmillan, Basingstoke, 1989)

CLINTON, B. and GORE, A., *Putting People First* (Times Books, New York, 1992)

CLULOW, C., *To Have and to Hold* (Aberdeen University Press, Aberdeen, 1982)

CONRAN, S., *Superwoman in Action* (Penguin Books, London, 1979)

CONRAN, S., *Superwoman: Every Woman's Guide to Household Management* (Penguin Books, London, 1977)

COOTE, A. and PATTULLO, P., *Power and Prejudice: Women and Politics* (Weidenfeld & Nicolson, London, 1990)

DAVIS, G. and MURCH, M., *Grounds for Divorce* (Clarendon Press, Oxford, 1988)

DENIS, H., HENRIQUES, E. and SLAUGHTER, C., *Coal Is Our Life* (Eyre & Spottiswoode, London, 1956)

DICKENS, L., *Whose Flexibility?* (Institute of Employment Rights, 1992)

DORMER, D., *The Relationship Revolution* (One Plus One, London, 1992)

DRAKE, B., *Women in Trade Unions* (Virago Press, London, 1984)

EDWARDS, J., *The Family and Change* (Knopf, New York, 1969)

FALUDI, S., *Backlash: The Undeclared War Against Women* (Chatto & Windus, London, 1992)

FOLLIS, P., *Ladies Elect* (Oxford University Press, Oxford, 1987)

FRENCH, S., (ed.), *Becoming a Father* (Virago Press, London, 1992)

GARRETT, J., *Does Parliament Work?* (Gollancz, London, 1992)

GIDDENS, A., *The Transformation of Intimacy* (Polity Press, London, 1992)

GIEVE, K., (ed.), *Balancing Acts: On Being a Mother* (Virago Press, London, 1989)

GORER, G., *Exploring English Character* (Cresset Press, London 1955)

GORER, G., *Sex and Marriage in England Today* (Cox & Wyman, London, 1971)

HANDY, C., *The Age of Unreason* (Century Hutchinson, London, 1989)

HEWITT, P., *About Time* (IPPR/Rivers Orams Press, London, 1992)

HEWLETT, S., *When the Bough Breaks The Cost of Neglecting Our Children* (Basic Books, 1991)

HOCHSCHILD, A.,*The Second Shift* (Viking Penguin, New York, 1989)

LEWIS, C. and O'BRIEN, M. (eds.), *Reassessing Fatherhood* (Sage Publications,]. 1987)

LUNDBERG, F. and FARNHAM, M., *Modern Woman: The Lost Sex* (Harper & Bros, New York, 1947)

MACLEAN, J. and EEKELAR,]., *Children and Divorce* (SSRC, London, 1983)

MANSFIELD, P. and COLLARD, J., *The Beginning of the Rest of Your Life* (Macmillan, London, 1988)

MCCGWIRE, S., *Best Companies for Women* (Pandora, London, 1992)

MOSS, P. and MELHUISH, *, *Day Care for Young Children* (Routledge, London, 1990)

MOSSE, K., *Becoming A Mother* (Virago Press, London, 1993)

OAKLEY, A., *Housewife* (Penguin Books, London, 1974)

OSBORNE, A. and MILLBANK, J. *The Effects of Early Education* (Oxford University Press, Oxford, 1987)

OWEN, R., *A New View of Society or Essays on the Principles of Formation of the Human Character and the Application of the Principle to Practice* (Cadell & Davies, London, 1813)

PRICE, J., *Motherhood: What it Does to Your Mind* (Pandora, London, 1988)

ROBERTS, Y., *Mad About Women: Can There Ever Be Fair Play Between the Sexes* (Virago Press, London, 1992)

RYAN M., *The Cradle of the Middle Class* (Cambridge University Press, Cambridge, 1981)

SAMPSON, A., *The Anatomy of Britain* (Hodder & Stoughton, London, 1962)

SEGAL, L., *Slow Motion: Changing Masculinities* (Virago Press, London, 1992)

SHARPE, S., *Double Identity: The Lives of Working Mothers* (Pelican Books, London, 1984)

SUMMERFIELD, P., *Women Workers in the Second World War* (Croom Helm, London, 1984)

TAYLOR, D., *Eve and the New Jerusalem* (Virago Press, London, 1983)

VALLANCE, E., *Women in the House: A Study of Women Members of Parliament* (Athlone Press, London, 1979)

VANCE, C.S., *Pleasure and Danger: Exploring Female Sexuality* (Pandora, London, 1989)

WALLERSTEIN, J. and BLAKESLEE, S., *Second Chances* (Corgi, London, 1990)

YOUNG, M.F.D. and WILLMOTT, P., *Family and Kinship in East London* (Penguin Books, London, 1962)

Index